OWN THE LADDER

I0492500

A No-Nonsense Step-By-Step Guide
to Owning More Money

STOP
Climbing the Corporate Ladder
and
OWN THE LADDER!

G. Edward Marshall

The Wealth Publishing Group
Teaching Prosperity

"Own The Ladder"

A No-Nonsense Step-By-Step Guide to Owning More Money

Published by:
 The Wealth Publishing Group

ISBN-13: 978-0-692-97023-2 (Kindle Edition)
ISBN-13: 978-1984174017
ISBN-10: 1984174010

© 2025 Update

Dedicated to my father Leland E. Marshall
who taught me in both word and deed
the value and benefits of work.

And to my wife Debbie who put up with all
my crazy business ideas through
trial and tribulation.

CONTENTS

FOREWORD

G. Edward Marshall has a special gift that entices the reader to not only think about starting a business but excites the reader to want to get up and be something more in their life. His steps to start a business are so well laid out chronologically, it's almost as easy as 1-2-3.

He uses everyday language so anyone can understand and follow the steps necessary to enjoy more happiness in their life. Not only has Mr. Marshall done his homework, but he has also lived the experience of how to 'Own The Ladder.'

This book is the answer to all those who think they can never afford to retire or are struggling through retirement financially right now. If I were 25 years younger, I might try it again using his guidelines.

Paul E. Berney
Vice President Sales & Marketing, *Retired*
Sierra Aluminum Company
Riverside, CA USA

October 2017

INTRODUCTION

This book is for all those who want to break out of their 9-to-5 nightmare, leave the office politics behind and be their own boss. I have worked both as an employee and as a business owner. Being the business owner is by far the better way to go.

I have endeavored to write this book using stories and my own real-world experiences to keep you engaged and motivated to become an entrepreneur. I write as if you were sitting next to me and I were teaching you step-by-step how to be in business for yourself. I use everyday language and have omitted the *ivory tower* platitudes and words so anyone can follow my steps to greater prosperity. I have started and operated seven businesses. Yes, seven! Four have done very well and the other three? Let's just say that I learned what **NOT** to do! You supply the *will* and the *action,* and I will provide the steps to greater *freedom* and *happiness* in life.

-- *G. Edward Marshall*

"The world is awash in money! Do you hear what that means? It is awash in money. It is flowing for everyone. It is like Niagara Falls. And most of you are showing up with your teaspoons."

-- Abraham-Hicks

en·tre·pre·neur

Noun

Old French, from *entreprendre:* to undertake

Old Definition:
A person who starts a business enterprise and is willing
to risk in order to potentially earn money.

New Definition:
Someone who is mad as hell and not going to
put up with all the crap anymore!

CHAPTER 1

The Illusion of Security

"The best way to predict the future is to create it."
-- Peter F. Drucker

It's been a productive, yet relaxing weekend. You were finally able to complete several of those tasks around the house that you've wanted to accomplish. You were able to get some rest, and you are now basking in the glow of a successful weekend.

Suddenly, the alarm goes off at '0' dark early.' "Oh no" you think to yourself. "Not already!" You slowly get up out of bed and stumble through the darkness into the bathroom to get ready for work. Yes! You're going to do it all over again. You drive through traffic to work. Oh wait! I should have said you *crawled* through traffic for an indeterminable amount of time until you finally reach the office. You park in your favorite spot and realize that at least the day is starting off right in the parking lot.

As you enter the office, you notice there's tension in the air. As you head to your desk, people stare at you and then quickly look away. Just as you reach your desk, your boss comes up and starts screaming and belittling you right in front of your co-workers. You try to explain that the customer changed the plans four different times in the same week. Then you tried to get their approval on the last change, but they wouldn't return your phone calls. You even went to their office to approve the changes but couldn't get past the front desk. Now, the customer has just called and is irate because the project is behind schedule and wants to cancel the whole deal.

As your boss's face becomes redder and the words become more demeaning, you would like to turn around and say those two little words: "I quit!" But you can't. There are bills to pay, you have a son and a daughter going to college and your spouse's hours have just been reduced. What do you do? You stand there and take it, that's what! The anger is welling up inside of you as well as that feeling of helplessness in your stomach. Finally, you tell your boss you will call the client and try to salvage the deal before it all falls apart.

So starts another miserable week where you feel trapped again. "This isn't the way it was supposed to be" you think. "I was going to have a great job and eventually be the boss. If I were in charge, I would never treat my employees or co-workers this way," you say to yourself. There has to be a better way. Well, there is!

Why not start planning your escape now and start your own company? Instead of climbing the corporate ladder, why not *own the ladder?* The concept of working 9 to 5 is dead! Do you stay late or even take work home to finish? I thought so.

In fact, your boss or company owner may not even like you. You are an expense to your company. Many people are being let go from their jobs so others can be hired at a lower wage to do the same job with a larger workload. Millions of potential workers are standing ready and willing to do this and your boss knows it!

Also, your 401(k) is probably toast. Has your retirement fund grown or lost money since 2000? 2008? The 2020 Coronavirus Pandemic? The majority, if not all, of retirement plans have suffered through these major crashes. Add inflation, fees and the taxes that were always due to this mix and you may end up with only half of your nest egg. And that's if you're lucky. Rather than attempting to grow a sizable pile of cash speculating in the Wall Street casino for retirement, **why not concentrate on replacing your monthly income with a cash flow business that you own and control?**

I have learned that life is too short to let other people tell you what to do or when you can go home. Think about it. Generally speaking, your employer lets you go home at 5:00PM for good behavior each day, but you must report back the next morning at 8:00AM sharp! And if you are just one minute late, that one little item can come up in your next performance review. In case you didn't already know, your employer, in effect, determines where you live, what kind of house you live in and what type of car you drive. I don't want to give that much control of my life to another individual. I want to control my own destiny. Don't you?

Being in business for yourself means never having to make up stories to tell your boss so you can watch your child at a school event, begging for time off or jockeying with co-workers for vacation time. Do you really want to give up that much control of your life for 'security'? Most people with real security are either in prison or live in a socialist country. For that 'security,' they gave up much of their freedom.

As an employee, do you ever feel like you are just going through the motions of life? **Are you too busy working for a living to earn any real money?** It may often feel like you are working for your boss, the bank, the mortgage company and the government.

You're trapped. The game is fixed against you. Shouldn't there be more to life? Are you reaching your full potential or just running on the treadmill of life day after day? I believe you will never become really successful unless you enjoy what you are doing on a daily basis. If you enjoy your work, it really isn't work, is it? It can become fun rather than a punishment.

When you are in business for yourself and a problem does arise at work, you can look squarely in the mirror and say to yourself, "OK! You're in charge here. What are you going to do about it?"

That's a lot better than having someone demean you in front of your co-workers and tell you that "you are lucky to have a job here." Loving your work can mean all the difference in the quality of your life. Live life to its fullest. Become the real you that you know you can be. Start your own business.

Let's face it. There are really only three ways to earn money in this world. The first way is to own a business. The second way is to own real estate. The third way is to own investments such as stocks, bonds or mutual funds. Either you own them, or you work for someone who does own those items. "Oh, but I'm a teacher," you say. That is a business. "I'm a firefighter." That's a business. "I'm an office worker." You work for the owner(s). "I'm in the military." That too is a business. You see, life is made up of assets and liabilities. Owning your own business is an asset. Assets put money in your pocket. Liabilities, on the other hand, take money out of your pocket. Examples of liabilities are a car, boat, RV and credit cards. Even your house can be a liability until it is paid off in full.

By following the principles and steps outlined in this book, I will teach you how to build an asset, (a business) that can become a golden goose that will soon be providing you with golden eggs (extra cash flow) each month. Eventually, you can train others to do the daily work while you go and do more important things in life.

The world is rapidly changing. Maybe you are nearing retirement or are already there. I believe that the retirement concept of playing golf all day or sitting in a rocking chair on the front porch watching the grass grow is outdated.

Since many people are living longer,[1] it is becoming increasingly difficult to save enough for a 20–30-year retirement in just 40 working years. Think about that for a moment. Let that statement sink into your mind!

I also believe there is a crisis coming to America. Most individuals have not saved enough money to be able to enjoy an affordable retirement.[2] Almost 46% of people today are taking their social security benefits (i.e. check) at age 62, the earliest they are allowed under current law to do so.[3] Also, the cost of long-term care is rising and Medicare does not cover these costs.[4] Many people are working longer into their *golden years* out of necessity.[5] They have been trying to amass a large mountain of cash to live on in later years. Again, most people do not save enough. And yes, the markets have taken away much of their wealth in the last few decades. (Ala 2000, 2008 and the 2020 Coronavirus Pandemic). I have met many schoolteachers who have returned to teaching because they were "just bored." Yeah! Right! Rather than attempting to save a pile of cash, why not *'replace income'* instead? It's much easier, faster and more rewarding. Remember, your best investment--*is you*!

How the Wealthy Got That Way

Did you know that over 80% of wealthy people own a business?[6] It's true. They have created a cash flow enterprise that when organized and operated correctly will run itself. They don't have to be there to earn a profit. In many cases, they own a system. Look at McDonalds Hamburgers for example. In the past, they employed a system that taught teenagers how to run a million-dollar enterprise selling sodas and hamburgers. In the near future, the order taker at McDonalds and other such establishments will be replaced with a kiosk where you place your order and then pick up your food from a special window that only you can unlock with a special code printed on your receipt or downloaded to your smart phone. With the advent of food delivery services, you don't even need to leave the comfort of your home or office.

In today's world of the information age, you are no longer required to perform physical labor to earn a living. Author a book, create an on-line application or start a business and have others work for you to support yourself.

Starting and owning a business is a wonderful, exhilarating and also a frustrating experience. It's like having a child. You created a business. It's your baby. You brought it to life, nourished and babied it along. It can be your greatest joy and also your greatest frustration.

That's all part of the territory of being a business owner. Thankfully, the joy comes much more often than the frustrations. Owning a business allows you the freedom to do what you want to do in life. The benefits of entrepreneurship can be freedom, increased cash flow, extra tax-deductions and hopefully, more time for family. Owning your own business means you control your destiny and get to work at what you love. Look forward to it. It's exciting and rewarding.

If you're looking for the short cut to get rich quickly, this is not the book for you. In fact, there is no such book! In 5 – 10 years, how old will you be? You'll be the same age whether you are rich or poor. How about being richer than you are today? And yes, if you wait, you WILL be poorer. With the rising costs of health care, energy and inflation, EVERYTHING is going to be more expensive in the future. I have been around long enough to remember 29-cents per gallon gasoline and the 5-cent jelly donut. They no longer exist. The rising cost of living has increased these prices significantly. Yet, personal incomes have not kept pace with the inflationary prices we now pay and will pay in the future.[7] Do something about it. Start a part-time business IN ADDITION to your current job. Pay off those credit cards, pay down your mortgage and build a nice, comfortable cash cushion that will help you sleep better at night. That is why you need to read and study this book. Later, when your part-time business is producing a sufficient amount of cash, you can decide whether to stay at your job or jump out into the exciting world of entrepreneurship.

One of the best perks of owning your own business is employing your children in the business. Even a youngster can wash the company vehicle, sweep the floors, take out the trash, clean the windows or stock the shelves. No, this is not breaking child labor laws. This is about teaching your children responsibility as well as how to earn their own way in life. It is an opportunity for you to teach your children at an early age proper money management. Instead of buying them a bicycle, play station or even the clothes they wear, turn these into a tax-deductible item for you by paying your children a salary (which can be tax deductible for you) and then 'letting' them purchase these same items for themselves.

I have learned that most successful people have a drive within them to want more in life. Stop allowing life or other people to kick you around. Stand up and take charge of your life. Make your own way.

Don't put your hopes and dreams in someone else's pocket. Build your own pocket and then work at making your pocket bigger so there is room enough for family and friends to succeed with you. I believe that is the true definition of a great entrepreneur.

A number of years ago, a woman was being interviewed on television for the evening news. Her husband had just been laid off from his job at the Kennecott Copper Mine in Bingham, Utah. She said, *"We've been secure for 15 years and now, nothing!"* Was she really secure? Or did she have the 'illusion' of being secure? Most likely, it's the latter. Each day that her husband got up to go to work were potentially his last day at work. He was at the mercy of his employer and world copper prices.

There is absolutely no more exhilarating feeling in the world than being in control of your own life and charting your own destiny. That can be a real sense of security. Isn't that what you really want in life? This book will show you how to do it. This is what being a successful business owner can provide. It's the opportunity to improve your life, the chance to be somebody. Pay off your debts; build financial reserves and own assets, not liabilities. You should also be paid according to the value you bring to the company, not by your tenure. If you are going to work harder or are required to stay late to get some tasks completed, wouldn't you like to get paid extra for that work? Most employees and government workers are on a fixed pay schedule. No matter what extra work they may be required to perform, they will only receive a paycheck according to a specified pay schedule. And, if you are waiting for someone to offer you a FAIRER salary for all the work you do, you will be waiting for the remainder of your life.

Stop wasting your time. Get out and make things happen and you will be surprised by a whole new world that can open up to you.

By being in business for yourself, you get to call the shots, you are in charge and people work for you. Your earning potential can be limitless.

One of the biggest reasons I wrote this book is due to the most recent business I started. I work in financial services. As I have sat with so many families over the last several years, I have discovered that almost NO ONE is ready for retirement. Most people are living paycheck to paycheck and not getting ahead. In fact, most people are falling behind financially. Why? First is the high cost of living. Next is the lack of financial education related to how money works and how taxes are the largest expense for any business or household.

Think not? Check out the list of taxes the average American can pay and not even realize it in Chapter 5. In today's world, people need multiple streams of income. Starting a part-time or full-time business may be imperative in the economic climate of the future. Why do I say this? Let's look at some real numbers that may not be too pretty about a large portion of our fellow Americans.

A recent survey by the Federal Reserve asked respondents, "If you had an emergency and needed $400.00, how would you pay for that emergency?"[8] A startling 46% said they would have to either borrow, sell something or would be unable to come up with the needed $400.00. Wow! What an indictment against our current financial situation in America. Almost half the population would not be able to come up with the emergency money! According to this same Federal Reserve survey, it was happening at all levels of income in America. Even upper-income individuals were feeling the pinch in their pocketbooks. Another survey by the Pew Charitable Trusts[9] found that a full 55 percent didn't have enough money socked away to cover just one month's income in case of an emergency or job loss. In a nutshell, most Americans are "financially fragile" and "living close to the edge financially." For many Americans, there is too little income and too many expenses.

The fallout from the 2008 financial crisis or the 2020 Coronavirus Pandemic requires that we make big changes in how we go about life. Gone are the days of bling and excess where every suburban home had to be 4,000 square feet and every driveway needed a brand-new Hummer with 22-inch rims. Gone... or almost gone... are the days of sending your kid to the best-name colleges, no matter what the cost, to get a degree in "Gender Studies of the 18th Century Lost Tribes of the Arctic Circle." (Okay, I made that one up.) Sure, just having a degree *used* to make a difference. Not anymore. The rules have changed. The path to wealth no longer travels through a degree from a nameplate college.

Also, have you noticed that what you buy is becoming more expensive? It now takes more dollars to buy the same thing you bought just 5-10 years ago. In 1975, a cool $1 million dollars would have bought you a lot. Fast forward 50 years and you would need **$5,584,927** when adjusted for an average annual inflation rate of about 3.5%. That's just to purchase that same lifestyle in 2025. Even if you had $1 million dollars just 20 years ago, you would require nearly **$2 million today** to match the purchasing power of **$1 million in 2005**.[10] Incomes are not keeping up with our shrinking dollars. This is all the more reason to begin a cash flow business that you own and control.

A word of caution. DO NOT read this book and then do nothing. That would be a great waste of your time and energies.

If you read this book and then walk away, you'll be leaving a lot of money on the table for someone else to pick up and enjoy. There are business opportunities all around you right now. Start your own business and place that money into your pocket rather than letting it go into someone else's pocket. It's your turn. As you start a business of your own, it will require a different mindset. No more 9-to-5 thinking. Yes, there are headaches, but the opportunities to get ahead are so much more profitable. I am going to teach you how to start and operate your own cash flow enterprise with just an idea and a small amount of capital to begin. Your life can soon be exhilarating again. Are you ready? Turn to the next page and let's get started!

1   https://www.statnews.com/2017/02/14/living-longer-without-better-aging/
2   https://www.usatoday.com/story/money/personalfinance/retirement/2017/03/03/10-statistics-that- prove-baby-boomers-are-in-big-trouble/98526764/
3   https://www.fool.com/retirement/2017/05/22/should-the-average-american-take-social-security-a.aspx
4   https://www.medicare.gov/coverage/long-term-care.html
5   http://www.pewresearch.org/fact-tank/2016/06/20/more-older-americans-are-working-and-working- more-than-they-used-to/
6   http://www.nytimes.com/books/first/s/stanley-millionaire.html
7   http://www.pewresearch.org/fact-tank/2014/10/09/for-most-workers-real-wages-have-barely-budged- for-decades/
8   http://www.theatlantic.com/magazine/archive/2016/05/my-secret-shame/html
9   http://www.pewtrusts.org/en/about/news-room/press-releases/2015/11/18/pew-finds-american-families- ill-equipped-for-financial-emergencies
10 ChatGPT 4o - adjusted for an average 3.5% annual inflation rate.

CHAPTER 2

Believing In Yourself – Your Key to Success

"The key factor that will determine your financial future is not the economy; the key factor is your belief in yourself."
– Jim Rohn.

Let's start with the most important ingredient to success: Belief in yourself. This is akin to faith. Having faith in your own abilities. Faith that you can do this and be successful, no matter how long it takes. Next comes planning, discipline, and perseverance and of course work. Because you are working for yourself, you can enjoy having fun doing it. Isn't that the kind of life you would like to lead? Why not create a life you do not need a vacation from?

On the road to success, your *'will'* to succeed needs to be larger than the obstacles you encounter along the way. The obstacles are the things you see when you take your eyes off the road to success. And always remember, on the road to success, there are no shortcuts.

Let's first define success. What is success to you? It is different for every one of us. To some it may be money and fame. To another person, it may be the freedom to be creative and follow your dreams.

Still, others just want to be happy at what they do in life and enjoy the ride. I have personally found success to be the ability to create for myself the life I have imagined without another person holding me back.

Starting a business can be a great idea for many people. Why? I have a friend who works for a major insurance company. He works hard and earns a good living. My friend also has a smart wife who operates a small business from home selling handbags and jewelry. It may sound small, but she has enlisted other housewives to join her. They all sell items to their friends and associates. My friend's wife earns around $2,000 or more per month. Not bad! But wait! It gets better. The extra money she earns each month is going towards paying off their mortgage early. They have no credit card debt, no car payments and enjoy really great vacations each year. This is all because they 'believe' in themselves. They have a part-time business that generates income. How would more money *'feel'* in your life?

With those thoughts in mind, when beginning a new business venture, *start with the goal of building that business and hiring others to run it for you as soon as possible.* I cannot emphasize this point enough. This will allow you to go and do the really important things later on in life. You won't be tied down to a J.O.B. That stands for 'Just Over Broke.' Remember, if you start a business and are always doing the work yourself; all you have really done is bought yourself a job. By building your own business and hiring others to work on your behalf, you are building the proverbial golden goose. Chart your own destiny in life and choose freedom over security. You'll be much happier.

In 1976, there was a movie called 'Network.' It was about an aging newsman who was approaching a nervous breakdown. In fact, he almost had his breakdown while on the air. His mantra was *'I'm mad as hell and I'm not going to take it anymore!"* That's how I felt about my personal situation years ago while working as an outside sales representative for a large chemical supply company. I was tired of all the corporate politics and the outdated sales training I was receiving. I wanted more. I wanted freedom from the tyranny of my overseers and from the 9-to-5 nightmare.

Throughout this book, I will challenge you and encourage you to free yourself from the bondage of your boss and to go out and build something you can be proud of. As I have mentioned before, **your ultimate goal is to hire and train others to do the work for you so you can go and do the important things in life.**

A Faith Promoting Story

Before we begin our journey into entrepreneurship, I'd like to share with you a story written by Harry L. Wilson back in 1912. It's about a young man named **Bunker Bean.**

Bunker Bean was orphaned when he was just a child. No one wanted him, so he roamed the world in rags hiding from the things that scared him. He was afraid of policemen, riding (or falling) in elevators, afraid of situations, things, the future, even himself on occasion. In essence, he was full of fears. Because he lived his life this way, others would often make fun of him thereby confirming his fears. Bunker Bean lived in the attic of a cheap boarding house. One day, a false fortuneteller moved into the boarding house and began to tell Bunker Bean about the great karmic cycles that existed in the universe. He owned a book on reincarnation and explained that each person went through many lives during their existence. Bunker's new friend explained that in exchange for some of Bunker

Bean's money, he could discover who Bunker Bean might have been in a previous life. After considerable time and prodding, Bunker Bean finally agreed to give this false fortuneteller some of his money. As the false fortuneteller gazed into his crystal ball, the fortuneteller became very excited and could not believe what he saw. This fortuneteller explained that in a previous life, he, Bunker Bean, was the great Napoleon Bonaparte. Back then, Bunker Bean was not afraid of policemen. In fact, all of Europe trembled at just the mention of Napoleon's name. Bunker Bean was shocked! How could this be? What happened? Bunker Bean's friend explained that the universe goes through vast karmic cycles and that now this cycle was on the ascendancy and soon, Bunker Bean would be a successful person again.

With this newfound knowledge, Bunker Bean went back upstairs to his attic hideaway. He stood and studied himself in his old, rusty mirror. Suddenly, he realized that indeed there *was* some resemblance. He soon went to the local library and read every book he could find about Napoleon. He even found a picture in an old magazine of Napoleon sitting on his white horse overlooking a precipice waving his sword above his head urging his troops on to victory. Bunker Bean taped this picture to his mirror and looked at it as often as he could through the glare of the single light bulb hanging from the attic ceiling. Bunker Bean thought that if there were no more wars to conquer, he would overcome his fears and conquer the business world.

Slowly, Bunker Bean began to think and act *'as if'* he were Napoleon. He began thinking positive thoughts about himself and the future. This resulted in Bunker Bean appearing happier and more outgoing in his demeanor. His boss at work noticed this change and gave Bunker Bean additional responsibilities. Along with these additional responsibilities, of course, came more money.

One day as Bunker Bean was working, the thought occurred to him, "who was I before I was Napoleon?" That evening, Bunker Bean once again sat down with his fortuneteller friend and asked him to once again look into his crystal ball and find out who he was in a life previously to being Napoleon. Once again, as money was exchanged, Bunker Bean's friend did not disappoint.

"Why Bunker," said his friend. "You were Ramses, the greatest pharaoh that ever ruled in Egypt. The people loved you." With this newfound knowledge, Bunker Bean once again studied himself in the mirror. He decided to act with majesty, empathy and concern for others. He even went to a local tailor and had a suit made for him that made him look taller. Again, Bunker Bean's employer noticed the differences coming over Bunker Bean and promoted him several times until Bunker Bean was an important person in his company.

Then, one day, Bunker Bean made a tragic discovery. He learned that his fortune telling friend was a fraud. That this supposed friend had taken Bunker Bean's money and filled his head with stories. But a strange thing happened. While Bunker Bean was listening to this charlatan, Bunker Bean was filled with positive and uplifting thoughts of success and confidence. He had learned new, successful habits. Since no one other than his fallen friend knew that Bunker Bean believed he was Napoleon and Ramses, he decided to continue with his positive self-image. He was no longer afraid of policemen, elevators, the future or *things*. Eventually, Bunker Bean became a wonderful success in his life.

I have always enjoyed this story. By starting a business of your own, you too have the potential to enjoy greater success.

There's a famous poem that, in short, reads:

> I bargained with life for a penny, Only to find dismayed
> That anything I had asked of life, Life would have
> willingly paid.
>> -- Jessie B. Rittenhouse

Remember that a determined purpose cannot be stopped or hindered. Your thoughts will make or break you. Thoughts of prosperity attract while thoughts of poverty repel. It's all an inside job! Believing in yourself is all that matters. Now! Let's get on with *your* success story!

CHAPTER 3

Peter, Paul & Money

"Where Have All the Flowers Gone?"
-- Song by Peter, Paul and Mary, 1962

We often hear the phrase "robbing Peter to pay Paul." The real question is, "How much does Paul really need every month to survive?" Before you start your business, you will need to know exactly how much money it takes to run your household each month. This is your financial starting point. A good entrepreneur should know what the numbers of their business are at any given time. Your household income and expenses should be no different. Print the following form and, to the best of your knowledge, fill in all the blanks that apply to you to determine what it actually costs you to live each month.

Download the form here:

Estimated Household Expenses

Create Income 2 Retire™

Income & Expense Worksheet

Salary	
Rental Property	
Other:	
TOTAL MO INCOME	
EXPENSES	**Monthly Pmt**
Bank Charges	
Cable TV	
Cell Phone	
Charity	
Clothing	
Credit Card Total-From Debt Pic	
Entertainment	
Gasoline	
Groceries	
House Pmt 1st	
House Pmt 2nd	
HELOC	
House Insurance	
Internet	
Investments: 401k, etc.	
Life Insurance	
Medical Expenses	
Dental Expenses	
Subscriptions	
Postage	
Savings	
Telephone	
Vehicle Insurance	
Vehicle Maintenance	
Vehicle Pmt. #1	
Vehicle Pmt. #2	
Other:	
UTILITIES	
Electric	
Water	
Gas	
Trash/Sewer	
Total Mo. Expenses	

To the best of your knowledge, fill in the blanks with your monthly payment for each category. For those expenses that fluctuate, enter an honest average monthly payment.

Subtract your expenses from your income to determine your disposable income.

Total Income $ _____

Total Expenses   - $ _____

Disposable
Income   = $ _____

Was this a surprise to you? Most people never really sit down and figure out how much it costs to run their home. Are there some areas in your budget that you can go without, at least for a short period of time? Maybe it's time for the "B" word. You know. Budget! *A budget is where you tell your money where to go instead of it telling you where it went.* This is part of how wealth is built, but that's a subject for another book. Right now, you need to know how much money you must earn each month just to pay your household bills. In addition to this, when you go full-time in your new business, you will also add in your monthly business expenses to come up with a total monthly cash flow to finance both your household and business.

Remember. We are doing our homework here so that when you implement your business venture, the launch will go smoother, faster and with fewer headaches. Then, you will know how much it takes to pay the bills each month. This is where knowledge becomes power.

Marshall's Rule #1

My rule of thumb: When you can earn enough money to support yourself for six consecutive months in your new venture, it's time to make a decision about your full-time job.

CHAPTER 4

Entrepreneurship And Taxation

"When the legislature is in session, no one's wallet is safe."
-- Mark Twain

One of my favorite reasons for being self-employed is paying less taxes than if I were an employee. If you are an employee, Uncle Sam, also known as the Internal Revenue Service (IRS), is your 50/50 business partner. As an employee, you probably pay a higher tax percentage of your income than many company owners.

Please be aware that there are two tax systems in America. There is one tax system for employees and another tax system for business owners. As I said before, business owners typically pay less in taxes as a percentage than an employee. This can potentially put more money in your pocket. This is again one of my favorite reasons why I enjoy being in business for myself. As an employee, you work hard for your money, don't you? You are in essence renting out your time and efforts to your employer. At the end of each pay period, you earn a certain amount of money. This is your 'gross' pay. Your employer then deducts your payroll taxes according to federal tax rules and sends your tax money to the IRS. The difference is your 'net' pay. This is what you take home and live on until your next paycheck. This is how the majority of Americans receive their payroll income each month.

As a business owner, the current tax laws are much more favorable. As a sole proprietor for example, you also work hard for your money. But this time, you are working for yourself, not your employer. It feels good, right? Oh, but it gets better! You see, each month, your business generates a certain amount of income. This is called 'gross receipts.' This is the total amount of money people have paid to you for your product or service. Now comes the fun part!

From your 'gross receipts,' the IRS allows you to deduct the expenses incurred to provide your product or service. Expenses can include such things as gasoline, vehicle payments, inventory items, business insurance, business lunch meetings, computers, printer ink, etc. Once you have deducted all your expenses from your gross receipts, the smaller, remaining number is the amount on which you will pay your taxes. Let's look at an example.

Mike is in the plumbing business. Mary calls Mike and says her kitchen sink is clogged. Mike goes out to her house and finds that the tree roots in her front yard have grown into her sewer line and clogged the pipes. Mike unclogs the sewer line from the house to the street at Mary's house. She pays Mike $100.00 for this service.

Mike does this type of service 1,000 times during the year and earns gross receipts of $100,000.00. ($100 X 1,000 = $100,000) If you were an employee earning this $100,000.00, your employer would deduct your payroll taxes and send you your net pay. This *'net'* pay is what you would live on for the remainder of the year. Since Mike is a sole proprietor, Mike gets to deduct his business expenses from his *gross receipts* **before** estimating what taxes he will be required to pay. As was mentioned previously, he can deduct expenses such as his advertising, truck payment, vehicle insurance, business liability insurance, parts, checking account fees, legal and accounting fees, office supplies, printing costs, internet, utilities, office rent, mileage or gasoline and much more. After deducting these business expenses from his *gross receipts*, Mike pays taxes on the smaller remaining number.

Because Mike is paying taxes on a smaller number, he gets to keep *more* of his hard-earned money. Wouldn't you like to do the same? If Mike is working from his home, he may also claim a portion of his rent or house payment and utility payments as a legitimate tax deduction.

This **legal** tax system can put more money in your pocket. Refer to the following for an example.

Mike's Discount Plumbing Service

Example:

Gross Annual Receipts	$100,000

DEDUCTIONS

Advertising

Bank Fees

Business Insurance

Cell Phones

Charity

Clothing

Continuing Education

Entertainment

Gasoline

Gifts Given

Health Insurance

Internet

License Fees

Office Supplies

Office Equipment

Postage

Printing

Subscriptions

Telephones

Vehicle Payments

Vehicle Insurance

Vehicle Maintenance

Minus Annual Deductions	-$50,000

* Not a complete list

Taxable Annual Income	$50,000

WARNING: As an employee, your employer deducts your taxes and sends the tax to the appropriate government agencies. As an entrepreneur, YOU are responsible for making your quarterly tax payments. Remember to pay your taxes on time. If you don't, the IRS will be more than willing to tack on additional penalties and interest. A good certified public accountant can help you stay on the right side of the law.

Here is a <u>partial</u> list of available tax deductions
available to business owners:

Advertising	Legal Fees
Alarm Systems	License Fees
Bank Fees	Mortgage Payment*
Business Cards	Office Cleaning
Business Bond	Office Rent
Business Brochures	Office Supplies
Business Insurance	Office Equipment
Business License	Office Furniture
Business Lunches	Office Utilities
Business Training	Paper
Cell Phone	Payroll
Checking Account Fees	Postage
Computer	Printing
Computer Repair	Printer
Computer Software	Printing Supplies
Copy Machine	Parts
Charity	Rent Payment*
Clothing	Shipping Charges
Consulting Fees	Stamps
Continuing Education	Subscriptions
Desk	Telephone System
Dry Cleaning	Thank You Cards
Entertaining	Toll Lanes
E & O Insurance	Tools
Fax Machine	Uniforms
Filing Cabinet	Utilities*
Gasoline	Vehicle Payment
Gifts Given	Vehicle Insurance
Health Insurance	Vehicle Maintenance
Inkjet Cartridges	Vehicle Mileage
Internet	Website Fees
Inventory Supplies	

These **MUST** be for a legitimate business purpose. Always consult a tax professional for available tax deductions related to your individual situation.

Let's also say you are a salaried employee with a full-time job, and you receive a paycheck after your payroll taxes have been deducted.

If you started a part-time business from your home, in addition to your full-time job, you could use the same principles Mike used in his plumbing business to earn extra income and receive extra tax deductions. These extra tax deductions 'may' offset the payroll taxes you are required to pay as an employee. This 'extra' money you now have can be used to pay down credit cards, pay off your mortgage faster or enhance the quality of your life. Please consult a tax professional for your individual situation.

Are you starting to see the benefits of entrepreneurship? You are building the *'Golden Goose'* that can pay you *'Golden Eggs'* each month.

You may be thinking, "I will just go get a job part-time to supplement my retirement income" or you may decide to tell your spouse, "Honey, it's time to get a job." These thoughts may be the worst idea you ever had. Why do I say that? Please put this book down and go online and view the following video. It may be the most profitable eight minutes of your life.

Go ahead! Watch the video, then come back and let's get your business party started! The video is called *"2013 Tax Secrets by Sandy Botkin" at* www.google.com. The numbers are a little different in today's world, but the concept is the same. Or on-line at https://www.youtube.com/watch?v=TNPC7_FiE-g

27

Marshall's Rule #2

"Entrepreneurship can be the Golden Goose that produces your Golden Eggs."

* If you are working from your home, only a portion of these expenses may be deducted. Seek professional advice.

CHAPTER 5

Wait! I'm Not Finished Taking Your Money

-- Uncle Sam

As mentioned previously, if you are an employee, Uncle Sam is your 50/50 joint partner with the income you earn. Why do I say that? Under the current tax system, most Americans can pay up to 50% of their *'gross income'* in taxes. This is why so many people are finding it more and more difficult to make ends meet in today's economy.

Below is a <u>partial</u> list of taxes many hard-working Americans pay without ever realizing the extent of how much they really pay in taxes.

Accounts Receivable Tax	IRA Investment Tax
Building Permit Tax	IRS Interest Charges (tax on top of tax),
Driver's License Tax	IRS Penalties (tax on top of tax),
Capital Gains Tax	Life Insurance Tax
Cigarette Tax	Liquor Tax,
Corporate Income Tax	Lumber Tax,
Dog License Tax	Luxury Tax,
Estate Tax	Marriage License Tax,
Federal Income Tax	Medicare Tax,
Federal Unemployment Tax (FUTA)	Paint Recycling Tax
Fishing License Tax	Property Tax,
Food License Tax Fuel Permit Tax	Real Estate Tax,
Gasoline Tax	Recreational Vehicle Tax,
Hunting License Tax	401k Retirement Tax
Inheritance Tax	Road Usage Tax (Truckers),
Inventory Tax	Service Charge Taxes,

Social Security Tax,
Sales Taxes,
School Tax,
Soda Bottle tax
State Income Tax,
State Unemployment Tax (SUTA),
Telephone Federal Excise Tax,
Telephone Federal Universal Service Tax,
Telephone Federal, State and Local
Surcharge Tax,
Telephone Minimum Usage Surcharge Tax,

Telephone Recurring and Non-recurring
Charges Tax,
Telephone State and Local Tax,
Telephone Usage Charge Tax,
Utility Tax,
Vehicle License Registration Tax,
Vehicle Sales Tax,
Watercraft Registration Tax,
Water Bottle Recycle Tax
Well Permit Tax,
Workers' Compensation Tax

You may be thinking, "I don't pay many of these taxes myself." Every business passes along its costs, including taxes paid by the business, to the retail price of everything you and I purchase. In the end, the consumer pays for everything.

Not one of these taxes existed 100 years ago and there was prosperity, absolutely no national debt, and the largest middle class in the world and Mom stayed home to raise the kids.

CHAPTER 6

Step 1: The Idea

"Thinking is the hardest work there is. That
is why so few people engage in it."
-- Henry Ford

Now that you've decided to be your own boss, the first step is to decide what you are going to do for other people that will cause them to pay for your service, product or idea. If you want to be a business owner, but you are not sure what to do or you would like someone to hold your hand along the way, choose a mentor, a franchise or a relationship marketing organization. (Amway, Avon, etc.)

When I started my first enterprise, I wanted to earn more money and have more freedom. I began with something I already knew. It was a service business. I knew my craft and I enjoyed dealing with people. It's much easier to begin with something you already know how to do. Here's a secret: Do something you <u>love</u> to do. Something you have a passion for doing.

If you're going to work, why not work at something you enjoy while getting paid to do it? And of course, can you earn enough money in the long term to quit your regular job?

When deciding what kind of business to get into, first look inward. Ask yourself questions such as:

- What am I good at doing?
- What talents or abilities do I have?
- What service can I perform, or knowledge can I impart that people would be willing to pay for?
- Am I a people person?

I strongly feel that everyone should learn a trade. What do I mean by a 'trade'? Plumbing, house framing, electrical work, computer repair and insurance are good examples. Having experience in more than one field opens up additional opportunities to earn extra income. Start with what you know.

If you want to be in business for yourself, but you are still drawing a blank about which direction to go, following is a list of possible businesses you could start that may stimulate your thinking.

Download this form here:

Partial List of Possible Start-Up Businesses

Accountant
Adult Daycare
Advertising
Air Conditioning
Antique Dealer
Appraiser
Arborist
Architect
Artist/Artist Supply
Auctioneer
Audio/Visual Service
Auditor
Auto Detail
Auto Mechanic
Baker
Beauty Salon/Supply
Beverage Distributor
Bodyguard Service
Candy Maker/Store
Carpenter
Carpet/Flooring
Carpet Cleaning
Catering Service
Check Cashing
Childcare/After School
Clothing Store Owner
Coffee Delivery Service
Computer Consultant
Computer Repair
Contract Writer
Consultant
Delivery Service
Designer
Diesel Repair
Direct Mail Service
Donut Store
Drywall Repair
Electrician
Employment Agency
Engineer
Errand Service
Farmer
Flood/Fire Repair
Florist
Foreclosures

Franchise Owner
Fund Raiser
General Contractor
Granite Countertops
Graphic Design
Grocery Store
Handyman
Health Care
Heating & Cooling
Home Healthcare
Home Inspector
House Cleaning
House Sitter
Import-Export
Insurance Agent
Interior Decorator
Janitorial Service
Janitorial Supply
Jewelry Repair
Jewelry Sales
Laundromat
Landscaping
Lawn Care
Lawn Fertilizing
Lecturer
Limousine Service
Long-Term Care
Machinist
Management Consultant
Marketing Service
Medical Transportation
Mobile Home Repair
Mobile Income Tax
Moving & Storage
Music Teacher
Networks Specialist
Newsletter Writer
Notary
Nursing Home
Office Machines
Office Supply
Painting
Party Planner
Pest Control
Pet Sitting

Petting Zoo
Photographer
Pilot Car Service
Pizza Restaurant
Plumbing
Pool Cleaning / Repair
Pooper Scooper
PO Box Store
Pressure Washing
Printing Service
Private Tutor
Property Manager
Public Relations
Publisher
Real Estate Agent
Roofing Contractor
Sales Rep
Salvage/Scrap Metal
Sand Blasting
Sandwich/Deli Store
Santa Claus
Screen Printing
Screen Repair Service
Security Service
Service Station Owner
Ship/Boat Repair/Sales
Sign Maker/Service
Smart Phone Tutor
Social Media
Tax Preparation
Tool Supply
Trash Can Cleaning
Travel Agency
Tree Trimming
Used Car Sales
Vehicle Parts Store
Water Delivery Service
Wedding Planner
Welding Contractor
Welding Supply
Wholesale Distributor
Window/Glass Repair
Window Washing
Yard Clean Up

If you still cannot find something you think you might enjoy doing and could possibly get paid for doing it, find an old telephone book. You know, one of those books no one uses anymore except for maybe a doorstop? Open the yellow pages and look at the index. Run your finger down the pages and notice all the services and businesses listed. Choose a field or career that may be of interest to you.

Make a list and then seriously place a number from 1 to 3 next to each possibility. Number 1 means very interested, number 2 for somewhat interested and number 3 for a maybe. Make a list of all of those possibilities you have marked with the number 1. These are the areas you will ponder over first. Could those business ideas you have marked with a number 2 or number 3 be incorporated with your number 1 ideas?

Once you have decided which path you will embark upon, pause and give your decision a few days to settle and percolate in your subconscious. Listen to your subconscious. At some point in the near future, your mind will provide you with additional items to consider. You may wake up in the middle of the night or be watching a television show when your subconscious mind will say, "Ok. Here's your answer."

Once you have decided what service or product you will be providing, research what it's going to take to start a business performing your choice. As mentioned earlier, if your start up is something you already know, then you most likely know what you will need to open your doors.

With all that having been said, it's time to do your homework. This is one of the most important parts of a business start-up. It's called the 'planning and research' stage. This is where you gather the necessary information to make an intelligent and wise decision.

- How long will it take to get started?
- How much money will you need to start?
- Will you begin from your home, or will you need an office or warehouse?
- Are there any special licenses or permits you will need?

First, make a list of all the equipment, supplies and inventory you will need to start. Then, write down the cost of each item. Part of the process of starting your own business is to determine how much it is going to cost you to begin and what kind of inventory, if any, are you going to need? Every business is different. Some businesses require a few items at start up and others will need more to get started.

Ask yourself questions such as: Is it something I can begin part-time? Am I physically able to do it? Are there any special licenses or permits I will need? What kind of equipment am I going to need? Will I need a special vehicle? Tools? Am I going to need a computer, printer, catalogs or brochures? Will I use my home phone, my cell phone or a new number? Refer to the list on the following page to assist you in calculating what you will need to start your new venture and what it will cost you up front.

Estimated Start-Up Costs

 Download this form here:

Expense	Cost
Advertising	
Bank Charges	
Cell Phone	
Credit Cards	
Dues	
Estimated Quarterly Taxes	
Fuel	
Gifts Given	
Legal Fees	
Licenses	
Permits	
Liability Insurance	
Vehicle Insurance	
Vehicle Payment	
Vehicle Maintenance	
Office Supplies	
Office Equipment	
Office Furniture	
Office Rent	
Postage	
Printing	
Fax Line	
Internet	
Work Clothing	
Utilities	
Subscriptions	
Payroll	
Payroll Taxes	
Workmen's Comp Insurance	
Toll Lane Fees	
Other	
Other	
Total Estimated Beginning Costs	

Total up the initial costs and determine if that fits your beginning budget. If it does, then you are well on your way to entrepreneurship. Chances are, you already have an idea of what you want to do. If, on the other hand, the start-up costs are more than you can afford, what items can you do without at the beginning? Are any of the items you need already around your home or is someone you know willing to loan these items to you temporarily? Are the items you need available on "Craig's List?" My daughter completely furnished her two-bedroom apartment for her and her two children for less than $300.00. People were either selling their items at low cost or just giving things away. I was amazed!

If you are short on cash, and most businesses are in the beginning, bootstrap yourself into your new business. Tell everyone you know about your new venture. Enlist their help in securing the items you need. You will be surprised how fast and from which direction these items will appear.

My first desk in a spare bedroom was a Masonite door and two wooden sawhorses for legs. It all cost me about $20.00 in 1978. I added a touch-tone telephone and an electric typewriter and *voila!* My office was ready to go! Thereafter, as your new venture produces cash flow, you can add the equipment you need until you are well on your way.

However, you may find that what you thought you were going to do originally is not as interesting or as viable as you thought.

Do you know someone already in the business that would be willing to help you get started? A mentor can be a great asset in getting your new venture up and going. Finding someone who has already trod the path you are pursuing can often mean the difference between success and disappointment. Most successful people are happy to share their knowledge with someone who is 'serious' about their chosen field. In fact, many successful business owners see their position as a 'calling' in life.

Why do I emphasize doing your 'homework' first? Let me give you an example. Because I speak Japanese, I had the opportunity to work with several Japanese businessmen putting together a joint venture in the United States. When I met with them to discuss how we were going to begin, they asked a lot of questions. A lot! In fact, they asked questions down to the smallest detail possible. After several long days of constant questions and information gathering, I eventually became irritated and finally asked "why so many questions?" They replied that there were many other departments that had to sign off on this venture and they wanted to have answers to everyone's questions back in Tokyo. I was still irritated because I thought we could just print some brochures, import the products and I would do the selling.

What I learned from this experience was that by doing the homework in detail up front, the implementation and the speed of how things grew thereafter was nothing short of amazing.

The old adage, "Find a need and fill it" is still true today. Keep your eyes open for an opportunity to fill a need that people want but is not being filled or addressed properly. Can you take a current business or concept and add value to it? That's what Starbucks did with coffee. They took an otherwise boring commodity that everyone purchased and raised it to a new level. Do not skip over this area of investigation. This preparation stage is so important. If you do your homework properly, the implementation will be much easier and faster.

WARNING! Do your homework in the beginning and you will have fewer headaches during the implementation phase of your business.

The important thing is to get up and going as soon as possible. We can all get more *'things'* and more money. What we can't get back is *'more time.'* One of my favorite sayings that I learned from my wife is *"Begin... the rest is easy."*

The term for 'doing your homework' in business is known as *'doing your due diligence.'* If, after you do your 'due diligence,' the answer is 'No,' go back to your original list and look at another Category 1 idea. Then, go down the list and ask yourself those same questions as before. "Will I start full-time or part-time? Should I begin in my house or in an office?"

When you have weighed all the pros and cons and you have decided upon your new venture, it's time for one more exercise. Go to the next chapter to find out.

Marshall's Rule # 3

I call it the '*7 Ps of Preparation*'

"Prior Proper Preparation Prevents Poor Pathetic Performance."

CHAPTER 7

Step 2: A Name to Remember

What's in a name?
Everything!

Now that you have decided what type of business to begin and what your monthly expenses will be, now comes the fun part. Naming your new venture. Giving your new company a name can be one of the most important things you will do to position your business in the minds of people. Calling yourself XYZ Enterprises tells your potential customers almost nothing about what you do. On the other hand, **Mike's Discount Plumbing Service** creates a vivid picture in the mind of your prospects. Keeping things simple can make it easier for your prospects to identify who you are and what you do. Before that happens, **you**, of course, must identify who you are and what you do.

Here's a simple exercise. In 10 words or less, describe what it is you do. *"I fix plumbing leaks and clean drains"* is simple and straightforward. This is called the 'elevator presentation.' You should be able to tell people what it is you do in the time it takes an elevator to reach the next floor. Fill in the blanks below:

The name of my company is:

_____

When people ask me what I do, I say:

_____

_____

Remember to keep it simple, descriptive and possibly fun. I have a friend who started a Website marketing company called 'Lemonade Stand.' The image of a young entrepreneur standing on a street corner selling cold lemonade on a hot day brings back memories of simplicity when things were fun. Be sure and have fun with this exercise.

Once you have decided upon a name, you will need to file an 'Assumed Name' or a 'Fictitious Business Name Statement,' depending upon your local area. This is usually accomplished by going to your local county recorder or the county clerk's office. Once there, you will need to do a 'name search' to determine if someone else already has the name you want. This is performed by looking up the name(s) in a computer. You can do this yourself for free or pay a nominal fee to have the recorder/clerk do this for you. Because someone else may have already 'taken' the name you have chosen, it's a good idea to take with you a few backup names for your new business, just in case. You can learn more about how to do this in the next chapter under 'Finalizing Your Entity Name.'

If you are going to begin as a corporation, you may need to file with your local Secretary of State's office or other governmental agency in your area. Be prepared for high fees. A good CPA should be able to assist you in this endeavor.

That's all there is here. We're keeping it short and simple. Now that you have a unique or descriptive name for your new venture, let's look at what type of a business structure would be best for you and your new venture.

CHAPTER 8

Step 3: Choosing Your Business Structure

Formal education will make you a living: Self-education will make you a fortune.
--Jim Rohn

Once you have chosen the field and a name that can bring you fame and fortune, you will next need to decide what type of business structure you will use to pursue your dreams.

WARNING: This is a very important step. There are several different types of business structures to choose from. I have listed the most common types of business structures with examples of their pros and cons. As laws vary by state, you may want to consult a Certified Public Accountant or other tax professional as to which business structure will work best for you in regard to taxation. You may also want to consult with an attorney to protect any assets you may currently own. Gather information from reputable sources and then decide which of these courses of action will work best for you.

Sole Proprietor

The most common legal structure is that of a sole proprietorship. It's the least costly way to begin a new business venture. The sole proprietor personally owns and operates the business. All income derived from the sole proprietorship passes through to the business owner. Likewise, all taxes, debts and liabilities pass through to the business owner as part of their personal liability.

The sole proprietor receives all the income. All your business-related expenses are also tax-deductible. These tax deductions are a major benefit of being self-employed.

As of this writing, many of your medical insurance premiums are also tax deductible as a business owner. You can also hire your spouse, deduct their income as an expense and enjoy the income. Of course, the spouse must pay taxes on their income.

The downside? As a sole proprietor, you also inherit all the risk. If you are slapped with a lawsuit, your home and other personal assets are also at risk. All liabilities are your responsibility. Once, while I was working at a project, my parked truck somehow rolled down a hill and very expertly knocked down a block wall at the end of the street. My vehicle insurance paid for the damage. If the damage had exceeded my policy limits, my personal assets could have been at risk.

As you begin, be sure to walk around with a big "L" on your forehead. (No, not 'Loser.') It stands for 'Liability.' A good **commercial liability insurance** policy is something you will definitely want to own as a business owner, regardless of which business structure you choose.

In everything you do, do it properly and think before you talk or act. As I said, a sole proprietor is the easiest way to start a business. However, later as you hire employees, you will want to consider another type of business entity. Remember, your goal is to build a business that will run itself without you being there. This involves hiring and training employees in how to properly operate your business. You also want to protect yourself and your hard-earned assets.

Advantages of a Sole Proprietorship

- A sole proprietor has complete control and decision-making power over the business.
- The sale or transfer of the business can take place at the discretion of the sole proprietor.
- Minimal legal costs or documentation to form a sole proprietorship.
- There are few formal business requirements or corporate meetings.
- Profits from the business flow-through directly to the owner's personal tax return, with IRS form 'Schedule C' attached for business deductions. (Woo-whoo!)

Disadvantages of a Sole Proprietorship

- The sole proprietor can be held personally liable for the debts and obligations of the business.
- The sole proprietor is at risk for any liabilities or damages incurred as a result of acts committed by employees.
- The sole proprietor's business and personal assets are at combined risk.
- The sole proprietor must file and pay quarterly tax payments.

Even with all the liability in your court, sole proprietorships are still the most common form of business organization by a wide margin. As recently reported, there were approximately over 22,000,000 sole proprietorships, 3,000,000 partnerships and almost 6,000,000 corporations in the United States.

Partnership

A partnership is when two or more individuals come together and agree to begin a business between them. I suggest that some key decisions need to be made BEFORE a partnership is concluded.

Who is in charge of day-to-day operations? Who is authorized to sign contracts with customers or suppliers on the partnership's behalf? Are there to be any silent partners? Silent or limited partners are those who put in capital to the venture but have no say in the daily workings of the business. Who will be the treasurer?

A partnership itself is not really a taxable entity. A partnership files an informational tax return known as Form 1065 and is attached to each partner's personal tax return. It lists the partnership's income and expenses, and the amount of profits or loss accrued to each partner. All income received by either partner is passed through and taxed similar to a sole proprietorship. All liabilities are pro-rated. This means that you are liable only to the extent of how much money or other assets you contributed to the business partnership.

Because of these issues, I highly recommend you find a competent attorney to write the contract or agreement between you and your partner(s). Because of my own personal experience within a partnership, I don't recommend it as a viable possibility. Yes, two heads are often better than one, but any obligation your partner(s) enters into, or mistakes made also obligates you as well. So be careful. Good friends in business can soon become not so good friends and may not be a good mix.

Advantages of a Partnership

- An added source of capital to start the business.
- Someone else with specialized knowledge or experience.

- An additional head to discuss business ideas with.
- Someone who can operate the business if you become ill or incapacitated.

Disadvantages of a Partnership

- Bad behavior of a partner can cause negative consequences for you.
- If your partner dies, their spouse or companion may become your new partner.

C Corporation

The most common type of corporation is a C Corporation. This is a for-profit, state-incorporated business. Articles of Incorporation must be filed, and appropriate fees are to be paid to set it up with the state.

The C Corporation is a very interesting business entity. It takes on a separate tax and liability identity from that of the owner(s). Inside a C Corporation, you pay yourself a salary. The salary is treated as a tax deduction within the corporation, and you pay the normal tax rates on your personal (employee) tax return. This allows the business owner(s) to be removed from personal liability for debts incurred by the corporation. If your business goes bankrupt or is hit with a lawsuit, the owner(s) personal assets are protected. Only the business assets are at risk. This is one of the biggest reasons many businesses choose to incorporate. Also, as a separate entity, a corporation can own property, make business deals or even sue another business. All of this can be performed independently of the owner(s).

Advantages of a C Corporation

- The corporation is a separate legal entity from the owner(s).
- Corporations can deduct corporate benefit health plan costs as an operating expense.
- If a stockholder dies or wants to sell their shares, the corporation may still continue.
- The owner(s) personal assets are protected against lawsuits or judgments.

Disadvantages of a C Corporation

- *Double taxation can occur if there are any* dividends to the owner(s) and are taxed again at the applicable tax rate.
- State regulations must be followed very closely. Failure to do so can cause fines or other legal hassles.
- It costs more to start a C Corp than a sole proprietorship or partnership.
- Annual stockholder meetings must be held.
- There are additional governmental regulations and hoops to jump through.
- Annual fees may be required to be paid to the state.

S Corporation

An S Corporation is formed similarly as a C Corporation. The owner(s) or partner(s) of an S Corporation are taxed very similarly to a sole proprietorship or a partnership. Income (or losses) are 'passed through' to the owner(s) on a pro rata basis in proportion to their invested capital and is reported on their individual tax return.

Advantages of an S Corporation

- Corporate losses can be passed through, and you may be able to deduct the losses from your personal tax return.
- Liability is to the corporation only.
- Expenses and or deductions can be passed through to the owner(s).

Disadvantages of an S Corporation

- Additional paperwork and rules to keep up with compared to a sole proprietor.
- Just as a C Corporation, it may be costly to set up and continue.
- You must be a U.S. citizen to utilize the S Corporation entity option.
- An S corporation's earnings are taxed, whether they are retained by the corporation or paid to the shareholders

Limited Liability Corporation (LLC)

An LLC, although a business entity, is a type of <u>unincorporated association</u> and is not a corporation. It is more of a hybrid of a corporation and a sole proprietorship. The primary characteristic an LLC shares with a corporation is the <u>limited liability</u> aspect and the primary characteristic it shares with a sole proprietorship is the availability of <u>pass-through</u> income and tax deductions. It is often more flexible than a corporation and it is well-suited for companies with a single owner. LLCs are popular because, similar to a corporation, owners have limited personal liability for the debts and actions of the LLC. Other features of LLCs are more like a partnership or sole proprietorship, providing management flexibility and the benefit of pass-through taxation.

The federal government does not currently recognize an LLC as a classification for federal tax purposes. Therefore, an LLC business entity must file either a corporation, partnership or sole proprietorship tax return. An LLC can also elect to be taxed as an S Corporation. Once the business is incorporated, the owner(s) can decide to file as an S Corporation, usually within 90 days of incorporation. You will need to file an IRS Form 2553. This will not create a different type of corporation, but it will change the way the corporation is taxed. With an LLC, you will file both a corporation and a personal income tax return.

Finalizing Your Entity Name

Now that we have waded through the boring, legal mumbo jumbo above, let's get this business party started, shall we? You've now decided what to name your new company and you've done your research and decided which business structure to operate under. Now it's time to make your new venture a legal enterprise.

Since the sole proprietorship is the easiest and least expensive business structure to begin, we will use this format in our example.

You will need to file what is called a 'Fictitious Business Name Statement,' an 'Assumed Name' or another form, depending upon your local area. Either filling out a form online or going to your local county recorder or the county clerk's office usually accomplishes this. Once there, you will need to do a 'name search' to determine if someone else already has the name you want. This is performed by looking up the name(s) in a computer. You can do this yourself for free or pay a nominal fee to have the recorder/clerk do this for you. Because someone else may have already 'taken' the name you want, it's a good idea to take with you a few backup names for your new

49

business, just in case. If the business name you desire is not listed, then hooray! Go ahead and claim the name. You do this by filling out the 'Fictitious Business Name Statement' form to begin the process of establishing your company name. This usually means providing your name, address, telephone number and what business structure you will use. (Sole proprietor, corporation, LLC.)

They may also ask what the name of the new venture will be, the names of the company officers, when the business has or will start and an emergency contact number. Be sure to complete all the necessary information. Once this has been accomplished, take the completed form and your checkbook to the recorder/clerk window. Filing fees vary by area but are normally under $100.00.

Publishing Your Legal Name

Not all areas require you to do this. If your jurisdiction requires you to publish your company name, the county recorder/clerk will provide you with a list of approved newspapers in your area in which to publish your new name. **Warning:** Large daily newspapers will often overcharge you for this service. I recommend choosing a small, independent legal newspaper that specializes in filing new business statements. This normally costs under $50.00.

You will normally have 30 days to publish your new name. This is your responsibility. The county recorder/clerk will not do this for you. In a week or so, the publishing newspaper will send you a copy of the legal notice that was published. Keep this copy in your permanent business records, as you may need this from time to time. Also, when you go to the bank to set up a new business checking account, the bank may ask to see a copy of your business statement and proof that you have published your legal name in an approved newspaper.

In today's litigious society, it is good practice to protect you and your assets. Just like the story of the Three Pigs, if you are working by yourself and operate as a sole proprietor, you have a house made of straw or sticks. If you operate as a corporation or an LLC, you have built a house made of bricks. Eventually, you will want to place your business and other assets in a trust. This is similar to placing a wall around your property to keep the big bad wolf (lawsuits, Uncle Sam) from taking what is yours. Once you have approved your business structure, it's now time to order business cards, stationery and other business forms. Woo-whoo!

CHAPTER 9

Step 4: Looking For a Rich Uncle

*"You can complain about a lack of money, or
you can do something about it."*
- Martin Hurlburt

Now that you've decided which business to start, what you are going to name it and which business structure you will use, we will next decide how we are going to finance your new venture. There are several ways you can do this. The easiest and most obvious way to start a business is from cash already on hand. If you have enough savings set aside, congratulations. If you don't have a pile of dusty money sitting around like most of us, there are other ways to get your new venture up and running. The following are a few suggested ways to come up with your starting capital.

401(k)

First, let's start with some cash you may already have and not realize you could use it. Do you have a 401(k) or IRA? Depending upon your plan rules, you may be able to swing a loan from your 401(k) or Individual Retirement Account (IRA). Check with your account administrator about the requirements of drawing a loan from your qualified plan. We're talking about a 'loan,' not a withdrawal. Once your business is up and running and producing a cash flow, pay back the loan as soon as possible. This is part of your retirement.

Cash Value Life Insurance

Do you have a life insurance policy with a cash value account attached to it? This could be a Universal Life Policy, an Equity Index Policy, a Whole Life Policy or a Variable Universal Life Policy. Consider a policy *'loan'* from this account. In many cases a 'loan' is tax-free and may never be necessary to be paid back in your lifetime. However, it is always advisable to pay back the loan as soon as possible. If you 'withdraw' funds from your policy, you may be required to pay taxes on any interest you may have earned. Check with your insurance agent or advisor for the plan of action that best fits your situation.

Many plans charge 3% - 5% percent interest per year for a policy loan. That's a lot better than what a 'bank loan' will cost you. It may make sense to 'borrow' *your* money to produce a cash-flow enterprise. If you don't have one of these policies, does a relative or friend have one of these policies that would like to generate a larger return on their investment? Then, you can pay them an agreed amount of interest until you pay back the loan. If you have a straight 'Term' insurance policy, there usually <u>is not</u> a separate cash account attached to this type of policy.

Home Equity Loan

Accessing equity in your home may be an alternative. As always, use caution when contemplating this option. A home equity loan adds additional money to the principal of your home loan and will need to be paid back. Always seek professional advice from a reputable source.

Venture Capital

We've all seen the television program where business owners seeking money for their venture explain their new idea to a group of wealthy individuals who are sitting on the stage. Some of their ideas are crazy and some of their plans evoke a bidding war among the wealthy venture capitalists. Borrowing from a venture capitalist may be a viable way of getting your new venture off the ground.

The positive side of this equation is an infusion of cash and usually a wealth of experience from your new partner(s). The possible negative of this scenario is that yes, you now have others who hold a major stake in your new business. You may have to give up some control of your company while you use their money. And yes, be ready to explain, in minute detail, how you are going to use their money and how and when you are going to pay them back. Tread carefully here!

Angels

Do you have a rich uncle or someone with cash that believes in your idea? Is there someone in your circle of contacts or acquaintances that would like to invest in a business venture while earning interest on that investment? These people are called 'Angels' because they usually come with less risk and drama than venture capitalists (or your mom!)

Sell Assets

The best way to start a new business is with your own money. Do you have large ticket items around your home that you could sell? Do you have items such as an extra vehicle, motorcycle, boat, or RV or quad runner? Instead of making payments on these items, turn them into cash by selling them and using the cash for your new venture.

Do you look at your 'toys' and think you are just not able to part with these items? Is there a way you could 'rent' these toys out and make a profit? Then, use the profits to make the monthly payment on the 'toy' and use the remaining cash to finance your new business. Be sure to buy liability insurance if you rent out these items. Another option is to 'pawn' your items for cash and then buy them back later.

Micro Loans

A 'Micro Loan' is where you borrow a small amount of money from an individual. These loans are typically in the $25.00 to $200.00 range. Maybe this is all you need to get up and running. I started my first business venture with $700.00. I borrowed $500.00 from my brother and the remaining $200.00 came from my own pocket. Start small and generate a cash flow of your own. Then, build momentum and keep going and never look back. Oh, the sweet smell of success!

Seller Financing

Maybe you've decided to purchase an existing business. Will the seller *carry the paper* for you? This means the owner will sell the business to you on 'terms' negotiated by both you, the buyer and the seller. You operate the business while paying the owner a set amount of money on a predetermined schedule according to the 'terms' you both agreed upon. This relieves you of having to come up with a large down payment and maybe the owner will stay on as a consultant to help manage *(keep an eye on)* the business. Or maybe the owner wants to take some time off while you manage the business on a trial basis. This is where the two of you can be very creative. Find out what the seller's hot button is, (their reason for selling), and solve that issue for them. **Warning:** *Be sure to put <u>everything</u> in writing!*

Government Loans

The 'Small Business Administration' (SBA) is a government-sponsored program to assist small and medium sized businesses. Loan programs can include those for women, minorities or veterans.

The <u>Small Business Administration (SBA)</u> 7(a) Loan Guarantee program is probably the most popular loan offered by the agency. It is their basic SBA loan program. SBA 7(a) loans are for a maximum up to $2 million. The terms of SBA 7(a) loans are 25 years for real estate and/or equipment and up to 7 years for start-up or working capital. Interest rates are based on the prime rate, the size of the loan, and the length of the loan. SBA 7(a) loans can be used for purchasing land or buildings, equipment, machinery or supplies; long or short-term working capital; for refinancing; or for the purchase of an already existing business. If the borrower has funds available from other sources, an SBA loan may not be granted. (Go figure!) This type of loan is funded through SBA approved banks in your local area. Check your local SBA office for a list of approved banks in your area. This may be a good way to finance your new start-up but be prepared for a mountain of paperwork and a lot of time.

Borrowing From Family or a Friend

You might ask a family member or a good friend, to 'co-sign' a loan for you. As a co-signer, they don't have to give up their own money. They are guaranteeing their personal name and/or credit that the loan will be paid back in the event you don't make the monthly payments. Put everything in writing, including all the terms of payback, the interest rate, and what happens if you default on the loan. Don't accept just a handshake, put it in writing. This will prevent any 'confusion' in the future. Also, paying back the loan and including interest is a great good-faith gesture, and it may save the relationship. Here's a suggestion to keep your friend a friend; use an outside loan servicing agency to write the loan agreement, collect the money and pay the lender (your friend or family member).

Partner Financing

Maybe you have a friend or family member who believes in what you are going to do. Ask them to be a *silent partner*. A *silent partner* is an individual who provides funding to the business as their only contribution. A *silent partner*, sometimes called a *limited partner*, will also experience less exposure to liability because they do not participate in the daily operations of the business. This means they have 'ownership' in the new business, but no say in the day-to-day operations.

When there is a profit, you may share this with them or agree in other ways to compensate them for their investment in the business.

These are all options to consider. See? Now you're getting creative. This way, you retain ownership of your assets. As mentioned before, the best way to start a new business is with your own money. No one is looking over your shoulder telling you how to run <u>your</u> business.

Establishing Business Credit

As soon as you start your business, you should work on getting a business credit record. Here are my suggestions for building your business credit: Get a business credit card and use it 'wisely' for your beginning business purchases. Pay off the balance each month as soon as you can.

Set up a credit account with vendors and suppliers for equipment, materials and office supplies. Pay off these accounts promptly.

Get a bank account and operate your business as a "real" business, paying bills through this account rather than your personal account. It shows you are *'for real'* and gives you credibility when you want to get a loan later.

Most new businesses use personal credit while they are starting out. However, using your personal credit for business can be risky. Using personal credit for business can put your own personal credit in jeopardy. If you fail to pay back your business bills, your personal credit rating can be affected.

Borrowing from a family member or friend? Check out the Internet for companies that offer pre-written contracts and service loans. An example would be ZimpleMoney.Com. That way, your friends remain your friends.

<No solicitation for insurance products or securities is offered here nor do we endorse ZimpleMoney.com or any other similar type of enterprise>

CHAPTER 10

Step 5: Creating Your Image

"Use a picture. It's worth a thousand words."
-- Arthur Brisbane to the Syracuse Advertising Men's Club,
March 1911

How you position your new business venture can be the difference between starting quickly and no one noticing you at all. I started a pest control business years ago called *Marshall Exterminating*. Most people understood what it was I was doing by the name. Yet, I took it a step further. When I began, I wore dark trousers, a white knit polo shirt with my company name embroidered on the shirt, a dark blue navy cap and a cell phone with an antenna.

I was once out soliciting apartment complexes to offer my services. As I was nearing the front entrance to an apartment manager's office, a young man who was sitting in the office saw me coming and only saw the word 'Marshall' on my shirt. With the dark cap and the cell phone with 'antenna,' he apparently felt guilty about something and assumed I was there to arrest him. He quickly fled out the back door of the office. As I entered the office, the apartment manager noticed who I *really* was and began laughing profusely. He called the young man back into the office explaining that I was indeed not the police. And yes, I acquired a new client.

Again, how you position yourself in the minds of your potential customers is very important. I suggest you create a *'Hook.'* What do I mean by a 'Hook?' A local carpet cleaning business in my area is called *"Pinks Carpet Cleaning and Restoration."* Their 'Hook' is *"If it's dirty and stinks, call Pinks."* Their vans and business cards are all pink! My *Marshall Exterminating* representatives handed out magnets with my name and telephone number in the shape of a sheriff's 5-pointed badge. Think of a *'Hook'* that you can use to create an image your clients will remember you by.

The old adage, *"Use a picture. It's worth a thousand words"* is still true today. Create a picture of what you do in the minds of people so they can understand what it is you do and will want to do business with you.

Sometimes, a company vehicle, brochure or business card will have way too much information. This can often confuse a potential client. Don't attempt to relate everything you know or do in your communication with people. Remember to be informative, yet to the point. Create interest in the minds of your potential clients so they will pick up the phone and call about your product or service and ask questions.

You will always want to keep a positive business image in the minds of your prospects. There needs to be a balance between a positive business image and overspending. If you need invoices (and most of us do) you can begin with invoice templates available from most office product software programs. These templates can be found on Quicken, Microsoft Works or Microsoft Money.

Many stationery or office supply stores sell ready-made invoice or sales slip booklets. I started with a form I typed out on my typewriter. I made multiple copies, placed a carbon copy paper between my two forms and put them on a clipboard. I was ready to go for just pennies. (Both the typewriter and carbon copy sheets show my age!)

If you think you can create a form yourself and want a professional looking paper to print it on, check with a local paper supply company. They carry many types of colored and pre- printed design papers you can put through a computer printer. If you have a few extra dollars and want to get extra fancy, go to www.paperdirect.com. They offer a large variety of paper frames, invitations, business cards, brochure blanks, etc.

Marshall's Rule # 4

"Act and look like a professional businessperson and people will assume you are."

> One of my favorites for invoices and keeping track of who owes me money is My Invoices & Estimates® Deluxe 10. Go to Avanquest.com and choose the 'Business' tab.

> Visit https://www.deluxe.com/shopdeluxe/ They can print almost anything you need for a business. Or use a professional printing company from your mastermind group.

CHAPTER 11

Step 6: Promoting Your New Venture

The greatest security is to plan and act and take the risk that will ultimately ensure your personal freedom and independence."
-- Denis Waitley

Now it's time to prepare and structure one of the most important aspects of your new venture. Getting the word out to prospective clients or customers is a never-ending activity. There is what I call 'The Three-Foot Rule.' Talk to everyone you know within three feet of you. With a big smile on your face, hand out your business card and let people know what you do. However, do not walk down the street handing these out to people willy-nilly. That's a waste of business cards and your time. You are looking for people who are looking for you. Right? You need to position yourself where people will see you.

Always remember that the first item you sell is yourself. People buy YOU! There are several ways you can advertise your new venture. This is called 'Marketing 101. Examples include:

Warm Market	Website Marketing	Door Hangers
Networking	Social Media	Magnets, pens, etc.
Referrals	Constant Contact.com	Yelp.com
Yellow Pages	Business Cards	Google.com

Promoting yourself and your company should become second nature to you. As mentioned earlier, your elevator presentation should be brief yet create a picture in the mind of your prospect of exactly what it is that you do. It's the A-B-C of Marketing 101: <u>A</u>lways <u>B</u>e <u>C</u>ontacting.

Word of Mouth Reviews

This is by far the best way to promote your business. Having someone talk positively about you and how you helped him or her is a great way to build a business. We all want to be treated fairly when we need a repair or help with a particular situation.

My mother always told me to do a good job for other people. She said, "Do the job so well, you would sign your name to it." When doing work for other people, wow them with your excellent work. Then, follow up with a 'thank you' card. Maybe call them in a few days and ask if everything was to their satisfaction.

Most people appreciate this. Keep in contact with them periodically. They may need your services again in the future. Be sure to keep a list of people you have performed work for. Periodically send them a promotional ad or email about a special you may be offering.

Networking

Networking is a must in today's business world. Everyone is bombarded daily with too much information. Networking with other like-minded individuals and business owners who will refer you puts a positive light on your business and separates you from all the others. Cultivate relationships with those that I call 'gatekeepers.' These are people who know other people who may want to do business with you and can give you an introduction.

Let me give you an example. I call it *"The Wedding Mafia."* Jane and Richard are going to get married in three months. Jane goes shopping for a wedding dress. She shops around and finally finds the 'right' gown. In her conversation with the wedding dress shop owner, she mentions that she is going to look wonderful in her wedding pictures. Mary, the wedding dress shop owner, suggests she call a business associate of hers who does wedding photography.

Jane takes the card of the wedding photographer and makes an appointment to meet him. At the meeting, Jerry, the photographer, asks Jane what kind of wedding cake she is thinking about having at her wedding reception. Jane hasn't decided yet or even knows whom to call. Jerry gives Jane the card of a fellow business associate who operates a bakery there in the neighborhood and gives Bob, the baker, a glowing review.

Jerry also offers the business card of an associate, Lance, who is a DJ for weddings and parties. Lance, in his conversation with Jane and Richard, asks what kind of flowers they are thinking about for the wedding. Lance gives them the name of Cheryl, a local florist.

Jane is thrilled. She didn't have to go through the internet or drive all over town interviewing and choosing the people she will need for her wedding. She already has too many other things to arrange for her big day. Unbeknownst to Jane and Richard, Mary, the dress storeowner, is friends with Jerry the photographer, Bob the baker, and Lance the DJ and Cheryl the florist. They all work together to promote each other's business. This is a perfect example of the adage *'givers gain.'*

Your job is to establish relationships with other 'gatekeepers' that complement your business and you can refer to each other for business. This is also referred to as a 'Mastermind Group.'

Referrals

Referrals are the best kind of business leads you will ever receive. Treat these referrals and the person who passed them to you with respect. In most cases, the prospective client has already heard about you from the person giving you the referral. They have told the prospective client how good you are, and you should do the same when referring others. Always be sure to send a 'thank you' to the person who referred you. This helps to build the relationship with your 'gatekeepers.'

Yellow Pages

Many years ago, you were not a legitimate business unless you had a listing or a display ad in the local yellow pages. Today, technology has advanced. I have found that it is now easier to look up the 'yellow pages' on the Internet. That old phone book that is delivered to your driveway or doorstep is now either thrown away or used as a doorstop. It's much easier and faster to look something up on the Internet. Depending on your business type, printed yellow pages in the phone book may or may not be what you need. I have found that having a listing on the Internet as well as a simple web page can drive people to you and compliment your networking efforts.

Printed yellow pages are final. You cannot change the print or message once they have been printed or delivered to your door. With a web page and the Internet, you have the option of changing how your potential clients see your business 24/7.

Website Marketing

I'm a baby-boomer. I came to the Website marketing party late. I wasn't sure if I really needed a Website or even how to do it myself.

Hey! I'm an entrepreneur. No one can do it as well as I can! Right? Wrong! I found that my yellow page display advertising was barely paying for the monthly advertising bill. A younger person showed me how to put my company name on the Internet yellow pages and begin a Website of my own.

The cost was much less than printed yellow pages and my phone started to ring once again.

There are a myriad of Website services available. Speak with your friends and associates and ask for a 'referral.' Many Website promoters provide a 'cafeteria menu' plan to choose which services you want to set up at a very reasonable cost. Here again, look for someone who has expertise in the social media field. If you are short of funds, and most start-ups are, start small and work your way up to where you want to be in regard to your social media campaigns. Check out www.ClickFunnels.com.

Print Advertising comes in all forms. You can 'wrap' your car or truck with graphics, print brochures, business cards, postcards and other items to hand out. You can also do billboard, radio and television advertising. The list and methods are almost endless.

One area I have found not to be of value is the phone call I get from the local high school or bowling alley. They are 'inviting' me to advertise on their hand–out sheet for the local football game or information sheet before you choose your bowling shoes. Unless you are a local pizza store with a 'free' drink coupon attached, I have NEVER, and I mean NEVER received a return on my 'investment' with this type of advertising.

A Final Word

Throughout this book, I have used the term 'client' rather than "customer." Webster's Dictionary defines a 'customer' as *"someone you sell something to."* The word 'client' is defined as *"someone who is placed under your protection."* The key to building great business relationships is to treat ALL of those with whom you do business as a 'client,' taking them *"under your protection"* rather than *"someone you sell something to."* People will usually notice you going the extra mile and are more likely to refer you to their friends and neighbors. It's all about trust, isn't it? Look at what type of advertising other businesses in your chosen field are using. It must be working for them. Don't worry. Often, business starts slowly. Just be patient.

If you follow these steps as outlined in this book, one day soon, you will wake up and be hard pressed to get all of your work accomplished in one day. That's the day you can look forward to enjoying!

> Want an 'instant' mastermind group? Check out BNI.com. It stands for Business Networking International. It's the largest business referral networking organization in the world.

> A great way to keep business relationships alive is by using a service called *'SendOutCards.com.'*
> You can automatically send a thank you card or almost any type of card to your past or prospective clients. They will print and mail the card for you. It's a great service to keep in contact with people as well as a way to promote your business.

CHAPTER 12

Step 7: The Power of Delegation

"I would rather have 1% of the efforts of 100
people than 100% of my own efforts."
■   *J. Paul Getty – Oil Industrialist*

One of the most important lessons I learned from being in business for myself is that you cannot do it all yourself. If you try to do it all yourself, at some point down the road, you will experience that wonderful result of constant hard work. It's called *'burnout.'* Yes, in the beginning, it may all be up to you. But sometime in your career as a businessperson, you need to train someone else to do the daily work you are doing. A common misbelief among entrepreneurs is that *"nobody can do it as good as I can"* or *"it's just easier to do it myself than take the time to train someone else."*

I learned the following lesson several years after I had started my first business. I worked hard each day and came home exhausted. I soon realized that my income was not going to increase much past a certain point because there was only so much I could do by myself.

This answer was given to me when I was talking to a client of mine who owned a Baskin-Robbins ice cream store. It would be years later before I came to understand what he was saying. He said, *"I realized the other day that I can only serve up so many scoops of ice cream a day by myself.*" There really is a limit to how much you can do by yourself. While I was in high school, I worked in a fast-food restaurant. I started out at the drink machine and then graduated to the fryer and then to the grill. Finally, I found myself taking orders at the window and adding up the totals in my head. (This was long before 'smart' cash registers.)

If I had tried to do all of these tasks by myself at the restaurant, most of the customers would have gone away mad and not returned because of the slow service. (It so happened that my brother, two cousins and best friend ended up working with me. (Boy! The stories I could tell.)

The following illustration gives you a picture of what I mean.

The Power of Delegation

You - The Power of One All by yourself

The Team -
The Power of Delegation
"Let" others do it for you while you have a life.

69

The most important thing you can do for your business is to train others to do the work you were doing and then get out of the way. This allows you to step back and lead, manage and orchestrate what is going on. You teach others how to be a clone of yourself so you can leave and *'have a life'* instead of being tied down to your 'job.'

If you continue to stay a one-person show, all you have done for yourself is to have 'bought' your own J-O-B. As I mentioned before, that stands for "Just Over Broke." Is this why you want to go into business for yourself? Of course not! By teaching others and collapsing time frames, you can become financially independent faster than trying to do it all yourself. Believe me, I have tried to do it seven times. It doesn't work. Period! End of discussion!

Eventually, your new business needs to run and operate without you physically having to be there. Remember, you are building the Golden Goose!

CHAPTER 13

Step 8: Putting the Pieces Together

"Our greatest fear should not be of failure,
but of succeeding at things in life that don't really matter."
-- Francis Chan

 The time has now arrived to put your plan into action. It's time to strike out on your own and be the person you were born to be. Are you scared? It's natural to be afraid or unsure in the beginning. Don't worry. It's going to be fun.

Soon, you will look back and ask yourself, *"Why didn't I do this sooner?"*

You came up with an idea. You've completed your due diligence (homework) and decided what type of business to create. You completed your paperwork and now have a legal name. You know fairly well what equipment and/or supplies you are going to need at the beginning and how much it is going to cost. Your invoices, brochures and business cards have been printed. Exciting, isn't it?

Now it's time to begin talking to everyone around you and letting him or her know that you are open for business.

If things start out slowly, don't worry. Just keep going forward. You've made a decision to press forward. Have faith in yourself and your idea and follow through with your new venture. Many people try for a few weeks or months and when not much happens, they throw up their hands and say, *"See. I didn't think it would work."* It's the old adage, *"if you think you can, you can. If you think you can't, you can't."* Remember, have faith in yourself.

As time goes by, your business will pick up speed until finally you are on autopilot. Don't give up. See yourself in your mind being successful. Looks and feels good, doesn't it?

As you begin your new venture, you are going to make a lot of mistakes. That is a fact of life. You are going to learn what works and what doesn't. Congratulations! This is all part of the game. It's called experience. Experience is one of the greatest teachers of wisdom in the world, is it not? There is only so much I can teach you in this book. Some things you will need to experience for yourself. However, if you follow the steps I have outlined here, you will not make any fatal mistakes that will throw all of your hard work down the drain.

Babe Ruth, the great baseball player said, *"Every strike brings me closer to the next home run."* As you progress through your learning curve, you will make fewer and fewer mistakes until you rarely make any. That is the day to look forward to.

In our world today, people have been trained to study, graduate and get a job and make someone else wealthy. Because of this climate, there is a significant amount of negative misinformation about starting a business. When many people start a business of their own, they are often mocked and laughed at by those who have been programmed to never even try. So what! I bet that most of them fought to get into the company of their choice and are probably now fighting to get out. Let them laugh at you while you *laugh out loud all the way to the bank!* Persevere. Press forward in your goal of building a Golden Goose. It will all be worth it!

What sets an entrepreneur apart from an employee? Employees trade their *time* for money. Entrepreneurs trade their *ideas* for money. Employees are *problem* oriented while entrepreneurs are *solution* oriented. Most employees have *pipedreams* where entrepreneurs have a *vision*. Where employees *compete*, entrepreneurs *create*. Employees try to *avoid* risk whereas entrepreneurs learn to *manage* risk. Employees seek for *security* and entrepreneurs seek for *freedom*. Finally, employees want to be *comfortable* while entrepreneurs are comfortable being uncomfortable because they are in *control of their lives*.[1]

Now it is time to *'put the pieces together.'* This is where the rubber meets the road. This is where your 'homework' takes place. I have included a 'Business Start-Up Checklist at the end of this chapter. Start at the top of the list and work your way down. When you are finished, you are ready to start your new venture. Before you begin, let me show you how this can be done using the steps we have discussed in this book.

Let's start a business together. Did you read the first word in this paragraph? It means "Let us." Instead of me telling you 'how to do it,' let us build a business together from the very beginning.

Peter and Paul

Our starting point on our grand adventure will be to discover how much money it takes to pay our monthly expenses and run our household. Then, we will compare our expenses with how much money we are currently earning each month. By subtracting our monthly expenses from our monthly income, we hopefully will come up with a positive number. If the result is a negative number, meaning we are spending more than we are earning, we either need to cut expenses somewhere or hurry and get our chosen business idea up and running as soon as possible to make up the difference.

Household Expenses

Expenses	Monthly Payment
Bank Charges	16.00
Cable TV	59.00
Cell Phone	55.00
Clothing	30.00
Credit Card Totals	280.00
Entertainment	200.00
Gasoline	180.00
Groceries	440.00
House Payment	1500.00
Internet	49.00
401(k) etc.	150.00
Medical Insurance	218.00
Postage	14.00
Vehicle Insurance	150.00
Vehicle Payment	325.00
Electric	95.00
Water	105.00
Gas	34.00
Trash/Sewer	33.00
Total Mo. Expenses	**3983.00**

This exercise now gives us the dollar amount we will need to generate each month in our new venture so you can eventually either quit your current job or pay down expenses so you can enjoy a positive cash flow.

Choosing a Business

Next, let's decide what type of business we are going to build. After reviewing the 'List of Possible Start-Up Businesses' in Appendix B of this book, let's choose to start a Pressure Washing business. What can we do with a pressure washing business? We can clean residential concrete driveways as well as sidewalks and walkway entrances in front of stores and other businesses. We can clean the outside of mobile homes or trashcans at residential sites. We could even go to apartment complexes and clean up the trash that has spilled out over the top of the dumpsters and then wash out the area to minimize odors. Maybe someone needs his or her vehicle engine or other equipment cleaned. These are just some of the possibilities with this business.

Next, we will determine how much money it will take to begin this business enterprise using the 'Estimated Start-Up Costs' worksheet in Appendix C. Here is what it looks like.

Estimated Start-Up Costs

Expense	Cost
Open Checking Acct	100.00
Fuel	75.00
Licenses	100.00
Permits	100.00
Liability Insurance-Annual	500.00
Vehicle Insurance	150.00
Vehicle Payment	325.00

Office Supply	25,00
Printing	180.00
Work Clothing	125.00
Equipment	500.00
Estimated Beginning Fees	2235.00

The 'equipment' column included your pressure washer, garden hose, ladder, gloves and other business-related equipment to get you started. If some of these costs are more than you can afford at the moment, determine what you may be able to do without in the beginning. Remember, maybe someone you know already has these items and will let you borrow them for a period of time. Also, items such as cell phone, computer or office furniture were not included here. You probably already have these items and might be starting out in a spare bedroom or at the kitchen table.

What's in A Name?

Hey! Let's have some fun! What are we going to name our new business venture? Here is where we can get creative. Maybe we could call it 'Pressure Points Pressure Washing' or 'The Force Cleaning Systems," "Under Pressure Cleaning and Washing' or 'Strong Arm Pressure Cleaning.' For our business, I vote for Strong Arm Pressure Cleaning. A Strong Arm exudes strength and pressure cleaning tells people what it is we do.

We have performed our *due diligence* (homework.) We know how much it costs to run our life. We have chosen a particular business to start, and we have given it a name. We also have a good idea of how much it is going to cost to get this venture up and running. Now we decide where we are going to get the money.

Start-Up Funding

After looking at our monthly budget, we determined that we are living paycheck to paycheck and have no other money to spare to start our new business. So, we got creative! We spoke with a family member and convinced them to loan us $500.00. We next had a garage sale that netted us $800.00.

Fortunately, we were able to borrow $1200.00 from our 401(k) (which was about all we had in there.) We now have $2500.00 to begin our business venture. We owe $500.00 to a family member and $1200.00 to our company 401(k) plan, so we better make this new business work!

Business Structure

Since we are starting out by ourselves, we have elected to begin our business as a sole proprietor. We went to the local government office and filed our New Business Statement. This cost us $65.00. We next published our New Business Statement in a local legal newspaper. The cost was $50.00. Not long after, the legal newspaper sent us a copy of our published business name. We took a copy of our published New Business Statement and opened a business checking account known as Strong Arm Pressure Cleaning with $100.00 as our starting capital. We next went to our local city hall and applied for a city business license, which cost us about $100.00. Wow! Our business is starting to take shape.

Create Our Image / Hook

Since the name of our company is **Strong Arm Pressure Cleaning,** we came up with a logo of a strong arm raised to the square flexing its muscle. When people ask us what we do, we respond by saying

"I terrorize dirt with pressure and make things clean." Next, we purchased two pairs of coveralls for $60.00 and had our strong-arm logo and company name embroidered on the front of each coverall that cost a total of $35.00.

Getting the Word Out

Next, we sat down at our computer and used Microsoft Publisher or Microsoft Power Point and designed a brochure to hand out to businesses and other potential clients. It didn't quite look right, so we asked a good friend who was good at graphic design to help us out. I'm glad we did. Our friend put together a 'killer' brochure and even designed some business cards for us. We couldn't afford to pay them but found out they loved chocolate chip cookies. We baked five-dozen chocolate chip cookies, and our friend was in heaven.

We took our new brochure design and went to a local copy store and for $11.00, made 100 copies to use for prospecting and advertising purposes. We also used our friend's graphic design and ordered a minimum of business cards from Vista Print on-line for $12.00.

We then went on-line to https://www.deluxe.com/ and chose and ordered service receipts and invoices for Strong Arm Pressure Cleaning. Our minimum order cost us $146.00 and arrived in about 9 days. While waiting for our invoices to arrive, we went to Wal-Mart and purchased a box of Number 10 business envelopes, a clipboard and writing pens for $13.00.

Now comes our final step. After performing our due diligence and preparing our legal steps, we are now ready to use the larger portion of our seed money that has been held in reserve to purchase our large ticket items. We shopped around and found that Wal-Mart had a good intermediate pressure washer at a decent price. We also bought a garden hose, ladder, gloves, towels and other needed items. These all cost about $445.00. Then, just to be safe, we purchased a $500,000.00 business liability insurance policy to cover ourselves in case we damage property. This cost us $500.00 for the year.

Wow! Here we are. All our research and homework told us we would need $2235.00 to begin our new business. So far, we have spent $1537.00. We raised a total of $2500.00 from various sources.

By subtracting the amount of money we have spent to get up and running of $1537.00 from our original starting capital of $2500.00, we have $963.00 left over as our working capital. **DO NOT** spend this money unless it is for a legitimate business purpose.

Promoting Your New Venture

You finally made it. You are now in business for yourself. What a marvelous feeling! You now have in your hands the opportunity to begin your trek towards financial freedom and security. Now it's time to let everyone know you are in business.

Are you on Facebook? Send out a message that you offer a valuable service. Next, take your brochures and business cards and walk in and lay a brochure on the desk of the apartment manager and tell them, *"I just wanted to let you know that we are available to clean any areas of your property that might need a quick sprucing up. Thank you."* Before leaving, ask them for their business card with a smile on your face. You now have a name and a number for contacting them again in the future. Do the same thing with property managers. They usually manage multiple offices or residential properties. Also, as you drive down the street, be aware of the business and warehouse signs that show leasing opportunities. These signs will usually have a contact name and telephone number. Call and tell them what services you are offering and ask them for a mailing address to send them some information.

Go visit a local mobile home park. They usually have a central community center with a bulletin board. If there is an on-site manager, ask permission to leave a brochure or business card on the bulletin board. Remember social media. A simple Website or constant tweets may be all it takes. Also look to 'gatekeepers' to help you. These are people who do similar business, but not exactly what you are doing. Network with them. Take them out to lunch or over coffee and a donut and discover how your business can complement their business.

Using your brochure, business card or a postcard you had printed, leave these on residential doorsteps offering your service to clean the grease and oil off their driveway or clean out their trashcans. Please be aware that it is against federal postal laws to place anything in a mailbox. Penalties or fines can result.

Some Final Words

Do not expect any of the people you meet to engage your services immediately. You are laying the groundwork for possible future business. Most of the people you contact will not do business with you. But enough will do so to make it worth your while. Most businesses take time to build momentum. Be patient. If you currently have a job, continue working while promoting your new business (not at your job). If you find yourself unemployed, then your full-time job is to be out prospecting and contacting people from 8:00am to 5:00pm.

I too have been unemployed and out prospecting all day. It is the hardest simple work to do. My experience is that it will not last long. Stay focused and out contacting people and businesses. Soon, you will no longer need to be out knocking on doors. People will be knocking on your door for service. Just 'keep on keeping on' as the saying goes. You will be glad you did. Don't ever be afraid to give up the good to get something better.

1   177 Mental Toughness Secrets of the World Class, pg. 3, Steve Siebold, 2005

The Business Start-Up Checklist √

You should check off these tasks in the following order, where possible. Not all items will apply to you. Remember to start small and keep your expenses to a minimum. Begin with just what you need to get up and going. You can add the rest as your cash flow increases. Be smart and have fun. You are now creating your own destiny.

 Download this form here:

THE BEGINNING
> Decided Upon Your 'WHY'
> Belief in Yourself
> Positive Attitude
> Estimated Personal Monthly Expenses

STEP ONE
> Your Chosen Idea
> Estimated Start-Up Expenses
> A Mentor / Franchise / Friendly & Supportive Resource

STEP TWO
> Company Name

STEP THREE
> Finding Start-Up Capital

STEP FOUR
> Business Structure
>> __Sole Proprietorship
>> __Partnership
>> __C-Corp
>> __S-Corp
>> __LLC

Filed Your Legal Name

    __Fictitious Business Name Statement (Sole Prop, Partnership, LLC)

    __Articles of Incorporation (C or S Corp)

    __Publish Your Legal Name

STEP FIVE

Created Your Image / Hook

Uniform

STEP SIX

Business Telephone

Business Checking Account

Banking Software to Track Income & Expenses

Licenses Permits Insurance

    __Business Liability

    __Bond

    __Workmen's Comp

    __Vehicle Insurance

STEP SEVEN

Advertising

    __Business Cards

    __Sales/Service Receipts

    __Invoices

    __Envelopes

    __Brochure/Post Card

STEP EIGHT

Equipment

Product

Vehicle

Home Office / Office / Warehouse

    __Sign

    __Office Equipment

    __Office Supplies

STEP NINE

    Client Account Software for Billing and Payments

STEP TEN

    Opened an Account with a Supplier

    Joined a Networking Group

STEP ELEVEN

    Website with www.Clickfunnels.com

    Employer Identification Number (EIN)

    (For hiring employees) (IRS)

    Payroll Service

    Hire the RIGHT People

    Trained Employees <u>Properly</u>

Chapter 14

Stupidity Kills

"Let's pass this bill so we can see what's in it."
-- Nancy Pelosi, Former House Leader
Affordable Healthcare Act Legislation

It's been said that most businesses fail due to a lack of money. I feel that's incorrect. Lack of money is a symptom of a larger problem. What kills most businesses is stupidity at the management level. Many business owners begin earning some money and make the mistake of thinking this will continue day in and day out. So what do they do?

Either they start spending the money on fun things, or they think they can take some time off and the money will continue to roll in. The reality is that a start-up takes a lot of hard work, determination, perseverance and keeping an eye on things before it can run on autopilot. It also takes time to build. Cash flow is a fluid commodity. Some days you earn more money than other days. The amount of money coming in on a daily basis also varies day to day. Some days you collect a lot of money and other days no money comes in at all. It's an up and down reality. The problem is that the bills and expenses continue to roll in. You need to keep the pipeline filled with work and effort if you want cash flow to come out at the other end of the pipeline on a regular schedule.

I was once involved with a company that designed and manufactured intra-oral video cameras for the dental industry. You know, those little cameras the dentist puts in your mouth to make that little crack in your back molar appear like the Grand Canyon on the video monitor? I was involved as the senior VP from the very beginning.

We first had an idea. Then we researched the marketplace and found a need. We next found an *'Angel'* for our financing. Then, we searched for parts and equipment and began the design and manufacturing process. Sales soon began going through the roof. We started out in a garage and finally graduated to an office and small assembly room. We were having fun and making a lot of money. Then, a very interesting phenomenon occurred. The owner of the company began to have visions of grandeur and rented a spacious building full of plush offices, a lunchroom, assembly area, conference room and a grand suite for his office.

The expenses started to grow and the mood in the building changed. Instead of enjoying ourselves and making money, we were constantly being reminded that we had expenses and that we needed to increase our sales. The pressure started to mount. Then came the death knell. The company owner decided to bring his three children into the business.

Suddenly, there were three *'supervisors'* watching everything we were doing. They reported back to daddy that we were *only* working 9-10 hours a day, and we were *only* bringing in about $30,000.00 each per week in sales. The three children began protecting daddy and everyone else in the company became the enemy. Needless to say, after trying my best to keep the company afloat, it failed less than 10 months after my departure.

Keep your eyes on the goal of building a business that one day will run itself without you having to be there. Stay true to your core business and don't try to take on too much or go in too many directions.

Remember, stupidity kills! Keep it simple.

CHAPTER 15

Keeping Bread on the Table

"Sometimes in business, you have to be a bit of a bastard."
-- Famous rock star

Well, maybe not a *you know*, but it can sometimes be aggravating to wait to get paid. You can work hard at your business all you want. But, until you get paid, your business cannot continue very long. Always remember that **'cash flow is *more important* than profit.'** Cash flow helps you pay the bills. Cash flow is how you will pay your employees. Cash flow is how you purchase more inventory or supplies. It helps you keep your doors open *'one more day.'*

Each new start-up is usually starved for cash. When your customers do not pay you on time, you are essentially subsidizing their budgets. Is that why you went into business for yourself? Of course not!

Here are a few suggestions for keeping your cash flow coming in on a regular basis:

1. Make sure your clients know what your payment policy is right up front. You can verbally tell them, or you can have it written into a contract, agreement or on a service slip. Tell

your clients what services or products you will supply. Then, let them know that you expect to be paid in a reasonable amount of time. Usually 'net 30 days' if you have extended credit. Then, keep an eagle's eye on your receivables. (What you are owed.)

2. Offer a discount if they pay you cash at the same time you provide your service. Usually 5% - 10%.

3. Tell your clients they can deduct 5% from the amount owed if they would pay within 10 days of the date of the invoice. This is better than waiting the full 30 days. Be sure to watch out for those who may take advantage of this policy. Some clients will wait 25 days to pay and still deduct the 5%.

4. Let your clients know there will be a penalty for late payments. Maybe 2% - 3% for every invoice over 30 days old. Check your local laws. Also, you will need to determine if chasing after the extra late payment penalty is worth it.

5. Offer your clients a discount when they refer a friend to your business.

6. Be sure to always keep in contact with your best clients. Send them a periodic thank you card expressing your appreciation for their business or their timely payments.

7. If a client is good at paying you and suddenly, they get behind in their payment, give them a courtesy call and ask if everything is all right. Remember, 80% of your business typically comes from 20% of your clients. These are the clients you will want to spend the majority of your time serving.

I have found that being firm, but courteous usually gets me paid very quickly. On rare occasions, I have had to call the client and say, "I'm awfully sorry, but I won't be by next week because I haven't been paid as per our agreement."

It has always amazed me how fast the client can get on the phone and get through to the accounts payable department. The check is often in the mail the same day. Keeping an eye on your business means keeping watch over your expenses as well as your income.

CHAPTER 16

Take a Stand and Plant Your Flag

"If you don't build your
DREAM
someone else will hire you to help them build theirs."
-- Tony Gaskins

Well, here you are. You have read through the book and are almost finished, but you most likely haven't started on your grand adventure yet. You're afraid. You're not sure if you can do this. I'd like to tell you a story about two people who live in the same city.

Jim is a dedicated employee. He arises early every morning and fights his way through traffic to work with people he really doesn't like.

Tim, on the other hand, is in business for himself. He too arises early every morning and goes to work in his home office. He is able to see his children off to school each morning. Tim works with people he considers his friends.

Each workday, Jim does what he is told to do by his employer. He watches the clock and looks forward to his lunch hour.

He also finds it a bit disturbing having to negotiate with his fellow employees for his annual vacation time. He usually misses his son's after school football games.

Tim enjoys being his own boss. Even though it too comes with challenges, he is in control of his time and income. Tim has three employees and assigns them their daily work. They in turn help him build his company daily.

Each month, Jim contributes to his company's tax-deferred 401(k) plan. He looks forward to the day when he can retire from the rat race and finally be free to do what he wants in life.

Tim, being self-employed, invests the profits from his business into a smart money account and helps his employees do the same.

Jim works hard at his job. At the end of each year, he looks forward to receiving a tax refund check from the government.

Tim works hard at his business too. At the end of each year, he is able to deduct his business expenses from his gross income. This allows Tim to pay a smaller percentage of taxes than Jim does and provides Tim with more money for spending or investing throughout the year.

After fighting through traffic every night, Jim finally arrives back home to visit with his family and watch a sports game on TV for an hour or two. Because Jim is on a fixed salary, he often has extra expenses that cause conflict at home.

Tim usually spends time each night in his home office finishing up on paperwork and planning the next day's schedule. Because he works for himself, he is able to schedule more time with his family when needed.

Jim's employer pays him just enough to prevent him from seeking employment elsewhere. When a water heater breaks or the transmission goes out on the car, Jim pulls out his high interest credit card and pays for the repairs. Jim struggles each month to meet his financial obligations and repay his credit card debts.

When Tim has an emergency or needs extra cash for a business opportunity, he borrows from his smart money account at very low interest. Tim is not required to pay back the money he borrowed from his smart money account but usually does from the proceeds of his business. It's part of his long-term retirement plan.

Finally, after working almost 40 years, both Jim and Tim decide to retire.

Jim now attends sporting events with his son feasting hot dogs and beer in the icy cold, nosebleed section of the bleachers. Why? When the stock market experienced a large decline, Jim never heard from his plan advisor. His retirement nest egg lost a large sum of money (twice), and his plan has never recovered. Jim also learned too late that throughout his working years, taxes and fees have increased and are now taking a significant bite out of the retirement check from his 401(k). His retirement plan now looks more like a 201(k).

Tim, on the other hand, also loves to watch sports. Having worked for many years building a business and investing in a smart money account that grew during up years of the stock market and stayed level in negative years, Tim was able to purchase his own skybox at the sports stadium.

Tim's smart money account now allows him to withdraw a larger portion of money from his retirement account because rather than being tax-deferred, his retirement income is structured in such a way that it is tax-free. He now watches the sporting events from the comfort of his private skybox suite with his family, friends and clients while dining on fine drinks and Hors d'oeuvres.

Jim, meanwhile, is now forced to spend the remainder of his retirement years working again for an employer he does not like so he can 'make ends meet.'

Tim, on the other hand, spends the remainder of his retirement working when he wants to and traveling the world, vacationing with his wife and grandchildren. His *golden eggs* (income) produced by the *'Golden Goose'* (his business) continues to allow Tim to enjoy financial freedom.

This same scenario is played out every day in America. The question is: Which path are you going to choose? Will it be the path of making your boss rich while you struggle financially the remainder of your life? Or will it be the path to owning your own business and enjoying financial freedom where you call the shots and decide your own destiny? The choice is yours. Which path do you want in life?

Your choice here:

__ Work for a boss.
__ Be my own boss.

CHAPTER 17

A Final Word About "YOU"

"Who you <u>become</u> is the sum total of your thoughts and actions."
-- *G. Edward Marshall*

A Final Note

When beginning your own business, if you haven't already, you will want to begin forging relationships with CPAs, bankers, insurance brokers, printers, suppliers and other 'gatekeepers.' Napoleon Hill calls this your 'Mastermind Group.' These are people who have specialized knowledge about things you don't know or don't have time to learn. They can be very helpful and will usually cost you less to use their services than the cost of the mistakes you may incur attempting to do it on your own. Look to those people you know and how you may help them increase their business. If done correctly, they will in turn send clients to you.

Are there downsides to being a business owner? Absolutely. You may have limited time to see your friends or other family members as you build your business in the beginning.

However, after your business is built and eventually on autopilot, you can turn around and help your friends and family much more than you ever could have with just your old regular J.O.B.

At first, you may miss watching sporting events with your friends. Keep working. Maybe one of these days, you can purchase your own skybox at the stadium and then invite all your friends to watch the game live in a more comfortable setting. Now, doesn't that sound fun?

Go forward! Follow your dream, make mistakes and gain wisdom and experience. Next time around, you'll know the right course of action to take. Isn't that what regular life is about anyway? You might as well start your own business instead of building someone else's dream. Succeed modestly or greatly. Either way, you succeed.

When you first begin your business, take any job or contract you can. Cash flow is king. As was mentioned before, cash flow is often more important than profit. You heard me. Why? Because cash flow keeps your company doors open *one more day.*

In your new venture, just continue pressing forward. Even when you don't want to work, just keep working. For every action, there is an opposite and equal reaction. One of these days, you are going to wake up and you will have more work and customers to take care of than you have time for. Won't that be cool? Persevere and it will all be worth it. I know! I've been there and it works!

Most people wait until all their ducks are lined up in a row. Don't wait. Most people say "Ready, aim, fire!" If you do, you will never start. Trust me. I've tried doing that. It doesn't work. Don't wait to begin. *Ready, FIRE, aim* is the way to go. As a businessperson in my sixties, I have learned that you can usually get more money, but you cannot get more time. That's why I believe in *Ready, FIRE, aim.*

Give your new venture at least six months. If it's not working out, re-evaluate what you are doing. By following the principles outlined in this book, I promise you will make fewer mistakes and get to your desired destination faster and with fewer headaches.

Increased cash flow improves the quality of your life and affords additional vacations. This is what being a business owner can provide. When beginning a new business venture, I again implore you to start with the goal of building a business and **hiring others to run it for you as soon as possible. Then, you can leave and go do the really important things in life.** Did you understand what I just said? Again, go back and re-read that previous line again. It took me way too long to learn this concept.

When you start a business of your own, it will require a different mindset. One of the richest men in the world didn't get there with a 9-to-5 job. He did it by buying businesses. These were all cash flow enterprises. I'm talking about Warren Buffet of Berkshire Hathaway. I also want you to remember the last four letters in the word enthus_iasm_. They stand for "I am sold myself." Be the best you can be. Really believe in what you do. Solve people's problems. During my working years, I have learned that rather than out looking for success, it's better to attract success. Be the successful person you know you can be, and people will seek you out and pay you to solve their problems.

If you don't want to start a full-time business at first, begin part-time selling popcorn, balloons or providing a service. Earn some extra money to offset your current tax burden with your J.O.B. or even help out with that additional premium payment with your new healthcare plan.

Remember your 'Golden Hours.' These are the times during the day or night that you concentrate on working. These are your most profitable times of the day or night where you can earn income for your business.

Run your errands before or after work hours. As you fill the pipeline with work, eventually, revenue comes pouring out the other end. Don't let anything interfere with your 'Golden Hours.' Again, you are building the golden goose in your business so that eventually you can live off the golden eggs. Eventually, you will have enough customers to keep all of your employees busy, so you no longer have to 'work' for your daily upkeep. You can live on the golden eggs (income) your venture produces each month. Just be sure to keep an eye on the goose.

A number of years ago, I experienced that phenomenon I discussed in an earlier chapter. I began to experience 'burn out.' I had not yet learned the principle of building a business so I could let others perform the day-to-day work while I did more important things. I was trying to do it all myself. My health began to suffer as well as my relationships with my family. It seemed I never had enough 'time' to spend with my family. I wasn't able to do those more important things in life such as spending quality time with my spouse or children. When I was home, I really wasn't home. I was either at the computer working on the telephone with clients or just too tired to do anything. This is why I highly suggest you plan to grow your business with the goal of turning the day-to-day labors over to others as soon as possible.

I knew there had to be a better way. So, instead of planning ahead, I just sold my business, thinking I would come up with another business while spending quality time with the people I loved. This was a shortsighted plan. The bills were still coming in each month, and I had several business obligations I needed to pay.

After paying off these obligations as well as the taxes that were due after the sale of the business, I was left with not much to show for all my hard work. Soon, I found myself out looking for a J.O.B.

What took place over the next seven years was just stupidity on my part. I wanted to continue to be an entrepreneur, but I let fear enter into my heart. How was I going to support my family? Where was I going to get the money to pay the mortgage and so on? I ended up having five jobs in seven years.

Finally, after working my heart out and having nothing to show for it after seven long years, I decided it was time to go back into business for myself. Since I had done this in the past, it didn't take long before I was able to support myself adequately. After many months of working hard, I sat one evening thinking about how stupid I had been and all the lost time and all the headaches I had put my family through, attempting to avoid working hard and experiencing that 'burned out' feeling. Ironically, I did experience that 'burned out' feeling while working long, hard hours at someone else's dream.

At first, I thought about that poor decision I had made seven years previously to sell my business BEFORE I had a back-up plan. From the mistakes I learned during that period in my life and since then, I am now able to share with you what works and what does not.

It was truly a learning experience. I am glad that I learned the lessons I did, but I NEVER want to go through that again.

This is why I will implore you again and again to follow the principles I have outlined in this book so you will not have to suffer through and learn these lessons the hard way like I had to learn. I now enjoy a constant flow of cash coming in regularly, I am able to schedule time off when I want to be with family or just alone and I can even go home on occasion and just take a nap. I am now better off financially *because* I am in business for myself.

Remember that 'Entrepreneurship' is living a few years of your life like most people won't, so you can spend the rest of your life living like most people cannot.

I have learned for myself that it is truly better to **'Own The Ladder.'**

-- *G. Edward Marshall*

Appendix A

Estimated Household Expenses

Download this form here:

Create Income 2 Retire™

Income & Expense Worksheet

Salary	
Rental Property	
Other:	
TOTAL MO INCOME	
EXPENSES	**Monthly Pmt**
Bank Charges	
Cable TV	
Cell Phone	
Charity	
Clothing	
Credit Card Total–From Debt Pic	
Entertainment	
Gasoline	
Groceries	
House Pmt 1st	
House Pmt 2nd	
HELOC	
House Insurance	
Internet	
Investments: 401k, etc.	
Life Insurance	
Medical Expenses	
Dental Expenses	
Subscriptions	
Postage	
Savings	
Telephone	
Vehicle Insurance	
Vehicle Maintenance	
Vehicle Pmt. #1	
Vehicle Pmt. #2	
Other:	
UTILITIES	
Electric	
Water	
Gas	
Trash/Sewer	
Total Mo. Expenses	

To the best of your knowledge, fill in the blanks with your monthly payment for each category. For those expenses that fluctuate, enter an honest average monthly payment.

Subtract your expenses from your income to determine your disposable income.

Total Income $ _____

Total Expenses   - $ _____

Disposable
Income   = $ _____

Partial List of Possible Start-Up Businesses

Download this form here:

Accountant
Adult Daycare
Advertising
Air Conditioning
Antique Dealer
Appraiser
Arborist
Architect
Artist/Artist Supply
Auctioneer
Audio/Visual Service
Auditor
Auto Detail
Auto Mechanic
Baker
Beauty Salon/Supply
Beverage Distributor
Bodyguard Service
Candy Maker/Store
Carpenter
Carpet/Flooring
Carpet Cleaning
Catering Service
Check Cashing
Childcare/After School
Clothing Store Owner
Coffee Delivery Service
Computer Consultant
Computer Repair
Contract Writer
Consultant
Delivery Service
Designer
Diesel Repair
Direct Mail Service
Donut Store
Drywall Repair
Electrician
Employment Agency
Engineer
Errand Service
Farmer
Flood/Fire Repair
Florist
Foreclosures

Franchise Owner
Fund Raiser
General Contractor
Granite Countertops
Graphic Design
Grocery Store
Handyman
Health Care
Heating & Cooling
Home Healthcare
Home Inspector
House Cleaning
House Sitter
Import-Export
Insurance Agent
Interior Decorator
Janitorial Service
Janitorial Supply
Jewelry Repair
Jewelry Sales
Laundromat
Landscaping
Lawn Care
Lawn Fertilizing
Lecturer
Limousine Service
Long-Term Care
Machinist
Management Consultant
Marketing Service
Medical Transportation
Mobile Home Repair
Mobile Income Tax
Moving & Storage
Music Teacher
Networks Specialist
Newsletter Writer
Notary
Nursing Home
Office Machines
Office Supply
Painting
Party Planner
Pest Control
Pet Sitting

Petting Zoo
Photographer
Pilot Car Service
Pizza Restaurant
Plumbing
Pool Cleaning / Repair
Pooper Scooper
PO Box Store
Pressure Washing
Printing Service
Private Tutor
Property Manager
Public Relations
Publisher
Real Estate Agent
Roofing Contractor
Sales Rep
Salvage/Scrap Metal
Sand Blasting
Sandwich/Deli Store
Santa Claus
Screen Printing
Screen Repair Service
Security Service
Service Station Owner
Ship/Boat Repair/Sales
Sign Maker/Service
Smart Phone Tutor
Social Media
Tax Preparation
Tool Supply
Trash Can Cleaning
Travel Agency
Tree Trimming
Used Car Sales
Vehicle Parts Store
Water Delivery Service
Wedding Planner
Welding Contractor
Welding Supply
Wholesale Distributor
Window/Glass Repair
Window Washing
Yard Clean Up

Appendix C

Estimated Start-Up Costs

Download this form here:

Expense	Cost
Advertising	
Bank Charges	
Cell Phone	
Credit Cards	
Dues	
Estimated Quarterly Taxes	
Fuel	
Gifts Given	
Legal Fees	
Licenses	
Permits	
Liability Insurance	
Vehicle Insurance	
Vehicle Payment	
Vehicle Maintenance	
Office Supplies	
Office Equipment	
Office Furniture	
Office Rent	
Postage	
Printing	
Fax Line	
Internet	
Work Clothing	
Utilities	
Subscriptions	
Payroll	
Payroll Taxes	
Workmen's Comp Insurance	
Toll Lane Fees	
Other	
Other	
Total Beginning Fees	

The Business Start-Up Checklist √

You should check off these tasks in the following order. Not all items will apply to you. Remember to start small and keep your expenses to a minimum. Begin with just what you need to get up and going. You can add the rest as your cash flow increases. Be smart and have fun. You are now creating your own destiny.

- ☐ Your Chosen Idea
- ☐ Your Estimated Monthly Expenses
- ☐ Your Company Name
- ☐ Created Your Image
- ☐ Start-Up Capital $_____
- ☐ Business Structure
  - __ Sole Proprietorship
  - __ Partnership
  - __ S-Corp
  - __ C-Corp
  - __ LLC
- ☐ Filing Your Legal Name
  - __ Fictitious Business Name Statement (Sole Prop, Partnership, LLC)
  - __ Articles of Incorporation (C or S Corp)
- ☐ Publish Your Legal Name
- ☐ Business Telephone
- ☐ Business Checking Account
- ☐ Licenses
- ☐ Permits
- ☐ Insurance
  - __ Business Liability
  - __ Bond
  - __ Workmen's Comp
  - __ Vehicle Insurance
- ☐ Advertising
  - __ Business Cards
  - __ Sales/Service Receipts
  - __ Invoices
  - __ Envelopes
  - __ Brochure/Post Card
- ☐ Equipment
- ☐ Product
- ☐ Vehicle Payment
- ☐ Office Rent
  - __ Sign
  - __ Desk
  - __ Computer
  - __ Printer
  - __ Fax
  - __ File folders
  - __ Pens, Paper, Stamps, etc.
- ☐ A Mentor
- ☐ Uniform
- ☐ Positive Attitude
- ☐ Faith in Yourself
- ☐ Joined a Networking Group
- ☐ Opened An Account With A Supplier
- ☐ Banking Software To Track Income & Expenses
- ☐ Client Account Software For Billing And Payments
- ☐ Website
- ☐ Employer Identification Number (EIN) (For hiring employees) (IRS)

A partial list of available tax deductions as a business owner

Advertising
Alarm Systems
Bank Fees
Business Cards
Business Bond
Business Brochures
Business Insurance
Business License
Business Lunches
Business Training
Cell Phone
Checking Account Fees
Computer
Computer Repair
Computer Software
Copy Machine
Charity
Clothing
Consulting Fees
Continuing Education
Desk
Dry Cleaning
Entertainment
E & O Insurance
Fax Machine
Filing Cabinet
Gasoline
Gifts Given
Health Insurance
Inkjet Cartridges
Internet
Inventory Supplies
Legal Fees
License Fees

Mortgage Payment*
Office Cleaning
Office Rent
Office Supplies
Office Equipment
Office Furniture
Office Utilities
Paper
Payroll
Postage
Printing
Printer
Printing Supplies
Parts
Rent Payment*
Shipping Charges
Stamps
Subscriptions
Telephone
Telephone System
Thank You Cards
Toll Lanes
Tools
Uniforms
Utilities*
Vehicle Payment
Vehicle Insurance
Vehicle Maintenance
Vehicle Mileage
Website Fees

These **MUST** be for a legitimate business purpose. Always consult a tax professional for available tax deductions related to your individual situation.

* If you are working from your home, only a portion of these expenses may be deducted. Seek professional advice.

ABOUT THE AUTHOR

G. Edward Marshall was born and raised in Southern California. He spent two years as a Christian missionary in southern Japan. He has worked as a delivery driver, an outside sales representative, a pest control company owner, an intra-oral dental camera inventor, a Japanese Joint Venture Specialist and in financial services. He has served in leadership positions to many civic organizations. His passion is to help people start businesses and live a more financially fulfilling life. He and his wife have been married for more than 45+ years. They have four children and enjoy spending time with their eight grandchildren.

For more information or to download worksheets:
www.CreateIncome2Retire.com

We would love to hear from you. Your comments are welcome.
Contact us at: CreateIncome2Retire@gmail.com

G. Edward Marshall also has a version of this book tailored especially for those in or nearing retirement titled
"Create Income 2 Retire" available at Amazon.com

ACKNOWLEDGEMENTS

I would like to give a world of thanks to some special people in my life. To Russell Hardy who has been by my side for so many years and seems almost like a brother to me. To my good friend Paul Berney who has been a source of constant support and encouragement. To my best friend, confidant and wife Debbie who has stayed with me through both the good and the tough times and continues to be my biggest cheerleader in life.

A special thank you to Dawn Andrews at Mental Toughness University for allowing me to use some great quotes from Steve Siebold's book, "177 Mental Toughness Secrets of the World Class." Also, to Darren Scott at Hard Press Publishing for copyright use of "Bunker Bean." A special thank you to Larry Brock Esq., for his proofreading and positive critique of my original manuscript. Also to Nick Caya at www.word-2-kindle.com and his magnificent team for formatting my manuscript and cover design and uploading for publication. I highly recommend their services.

www.ingramcontent.com/pod-product-compliance
Lightning Source LLC
Chambersburg PA
CBHW071324220526
45468CB00001B/487